Mr. Curran first met James Joyce in 1899,
·ve· ʰot¹ ·d·nts at University
remained
˙ ·ich
˙tʰ · ˙· ˙ ·˙·ʳˣᵧ

JAMES JOYCE
REMEMBERED

C. P. CURRAN

1968
OXFORD UNIVERSITY PRESS
NEW YORK AND LONDON

© Oxford University Press 1968

Library of Congress Catalogue Card Number: 68-20359

PRINTED IN THE UNITED STATES OF AMERICA

To my daughter Elizabeth Solterer and to the
memory of my wife Helen

PREFACE

Parting from Miss Sarah Purser some years ago on the steps of Mespil House, she broached a fresh subject, for it was still only midnight and she was reluctant to face the empty house. She had been reading O'Flaherty's *Informer* and she failed to recognize in it anything of the Dublin she knew for nearly ninety years. Was it now a city of brothels and pubs? Of course most of the drawing-rooms she had known were closed. They began with her aunt's in Capel Street. There each year the chandeliers were taken down in preparation for the Parliament season and carefully cleaned, crystal by crystal. Of course, she meant Gratton's Parliament. She had known many men of letters and men of action. They were all—even George Moore—quite respectable and her friend Michael Davitt did not frequent pubs. Was the life of Dublin now centred in the Palace Bar? So she gathered from her *Irish Times*. 'But perhaps you do not go there and can't tell me?' She felt chilly and grown old.

I don't know what answer I made but, driving home, my mind turned on the many *Pictures of Dublin* written in the early 1830s, the personal narratives and the later novels from Sheridan Le Fanu and Lever to George Moore and Joyce. Just as the dead kings of France passed into the embalmers' hands and, being eviscerated, their bodies were laid in St. Denis and their noble and ignoble parts divided and distributed throughout the kingdom, so it was with Dublin. The men of letters bend over the dissolving and ever-renewing city; with honey and bitter aloes they stuff their disparate urns. What sarcophagus can hold its volatile spirit? Under which thimble the pea?

In post-war years tales of a turbulent city drew the cross-channel newshawks where also good food and drink were unrationed and talk ran free. The pub crawl was established and—to use a tiresome cliché —a new 'image' of Dublin created. Some old lineaments, however, persisted in the new frame. Presently the newshawks were reinforced by transatlantic expatriates from the prohibition period as well as by serious transatlantic researchers who have made valuable contributions to the study of Irish literature. In the centre of it all there emerged the mythical Joyce. Out of a few pages of his books, out of a few months of his life, out of the preconceptions, as I dare to think, of some of his commentators Joyce in relation to Dublin has been presented in a misleading light. So much of Dublin has been so vividly recreated by the artist that one readily imagines his vignettes to represent the whole. His early contemporaries know they were selective. The artist's omissions were deliberate, not being part of his design. How little, for example, does the Abbey enter into *Ulysses*? The theatre occupied a great share of his mind in his early days. But why should he develop a field already tilled by George Moore, one of his masters, or pursue the theme of his own 'The Day of the Rabblement'?

The pages which follow had their origin in my midnight conversation with Sarah Purser on the steps of Mespil House and in my desire to set down as much as I can accurately remember of Joyce without reference to outside sources. What I have to say has its only value in this independence. There may well be, therefore, inaccuracies, wrong judgements, and certainly the repetition of facts now familiar through other writers.

I have written memories but not memoirs and touched only lightly on the politics of my day. These are now radically and happily outmoded in the Dublin of today. But I have found an autobiographical element unavoidable and have diverged far from my original purpose in attempting to live over again in the climate which Joyce and I once inhabited, and to breathe airs whose currents do not obviously blow through his writing. Count Leopardi, whom I later invoke, thought that a man's pride should not extend beyond his town. I write in vindication of my town and generation and out of 'the attachment', which Edmund Burke approved, 'to the subdivision, the love of the little platoon we belong to'.

Some of this text in one form or another has appeared in *Studies* and *Vogue* and in *A Struggle with Fortune*, as well as in certain broadcasts. My grateful acknowledgement is made for the debt; but most of all I am grateful to Miss Sheila Murphy whose help in every respect has been invaluable, and to Mrs. MacMenamin for the index.

1967

FOREWORD

SOME years ago I read in a philosophic review, the title and date of which I failed to keep in mind, that literature that has magnitude comes out of tensions and that, at their most effective, tensions are produced during a period of transition in a community. Athenian drama, for example, came out of tensions produced by the transition from elementary religious conceptions to philosophical disciplines. Thinking of what used to be called the Irish Revival, this statement came into my mind. One can now see that this literary productiveness—Movement, Revival, Renaissance, or whatever we like to name it, had creators of a literature that has magnitude—William Butler Yeats and James Joyce. Was the community to which they belonged making a transition? From what and to what?

I think it was, and I think that the tensions that gave these particular writers their magnitude came from tensions produced from a transition from the nation to the State. The same transition was made forty years before when Norway, with Ibsen as its dominating figure, passed from the consciousness of the community as a nation into the consciousness of the community as a State. Yeats and Joyce show, as Ibsen showed, their stressful involvement in the political and social drift of their country. On the Irish side there was recognition of Norway's priority of accomplishment: Joyce's tribute to Ibsen is known; Yeats invoked his name in connection with the project for a national theatre. I should place the period of transition in Ireland between the Parnell epoch and the establishment of a national government.

Constantine Curran was an observer of these tensions. His boyhood knew—closely knew, as he came of a Dublin family of Nationalist tradition—the decline of a powerful movement and the rise of an astonishingly constructive one. He passed through the College that was the one most directed towards national affairs, knowing the contemporaries that were to be the personalities and the leaders in the Ireland that was coming into being. He became part of the social and intellectual life of the capital. He entered the office of the Supreme Court, the centre of the administration. All this made him, a man of inquiring mind, an excellent observer of the period I have indicated. And he could evaluate it all the better being a Nationalist Irishman and a good European well read in several languages and familiar with centres on the Continent.

The foremost literary authorities have presented us with a James Joyce formidable in his learning and literary accomplishment and enigmatic in his history. Constantine Curran's book gives us Joyce as a familiar figure. He meets Joyce on his own social and intellectual level: the houses, the teachers, the books that formed one student are part of the other student's daily life. Then the acclaimed European artist is united with the student who remembers the jokes and entertainments of his Dublin days. The title of the book is fitting: James Joyce, a person, is revealed in a person's remembrance.

Fitting, too, is the writing of *James Joyce Remembered*. It flows evenly but with emphases that bring us to attention. It has humour. Indeed, as I read it I have the feeling that I am listening to good talk in a Dublin drawing-room. As he goes on, the talker knowledgeably removes some mis-statements that are in the Joyce texts. Was the background to Stephen Dedalus's struggle as ruinous as Joyce makes it out to be? In his own abode, yes. Outside, no. He was not a man of visual perception, the talker reminds us. He is misleading about the appearance of the College he attended: the houses were dignified, and one had style; the classrooms were from a great house. The students were not dependants. They were the European students as from the time of Abelard, with discourse that gives liveliness to pages of *A Portrait of the Artist*. Several were to leave a mark on the formation of a new state, some on the history of their country.

PADRAIC COLUM

June 1967

CONTENTS

PLATES

PART ONE

Joyce at University College

MY first sight of Joyce was in a classroom of No. 87, one of the three houses on Stephen's Green which made up University College. Modest compared with Nos. 85 and 86, it is an agreeable red-brick house of the type characteristic of our Dublin squares, and this classroom was on the first floor with three windows overlooking the Green. The ground floor was then occupied by the editorial office of the *Irish Monthly*, the magazine edited by Father Matt. Russell which published some of the early verse of Oscar Wilde, W. B. Yeats, and Katherine Tynan. The rest of the house was devoted to such of our classes as did not meet in No. 85.

Our entrance was under the leaden lion by Van Nost which surmounted the porch of No. 86. Passing up by a well-worn, stone service staircase hidden away from the finely decorated main staircase of the eighteenth–century mansion, we reached our classroom. This particular morning the class—a First Arts class—was in English literature; the professor was Father Darlington, the Dean of Studies, and his opening words were from Aristotle's *Poetics*. It was the first lecture I attended in the College, and to begin with Aristotle seemed to be very right and proper and filled me with a certain academic conceit. Before the lecture was over my growing conceit was punctured. I thought I knew a good deal about English literature. Had I not, only a few months before, won the gold medal for first place in English at the Intermediate (Senior Grade) examinations? I thought, however, that the poetry shop had closed down when the Intermediate course shut the shutters with Tennyson. I was unaware that the business of literature was still being carried on there and then. The lecturer made some passing allusion to Stephen Phillips who had just published his *Paolo and Francesca*. 'Have any of you gentlemen read *Paolo and Francesca?*' he inquired, and then immediately: 'Have you read it, Mr. Joyce?' A voice behind me replied indifferently: 'Yes.' I looked round and saw my first poet.

I grew familiar with that figure in my next three years in College. In my eyes it did not change much in the next forty: tall, slim, and elegant; an erect yet loose carriage; an uptilted, long, narrow head, and a strong chin that jutted out arrogantly; firm, tight-shut mouth; light-blue eyes which I found could stare with indignant wonder and which were uncommonly like Lord Rosebery's as described by Crewe, 'at times altogether expressionless like the eyes of a bird. They gave an air of inscrutability and sometimes of lack of interest in the surroundings of the moment.' So he looked that morning. My friend Walter Callan of the Irish Bar, who was some years senior to Joyce at College, told me that his attention was first caught by Joyce's careful attire, more studied than the average; Callan was a good judge in such matters since he had it in him to become private secretary to the sartorially elegant George Wyndham when he was Irish Chief Secretary. When Joyce had taken his degree, and as his family circumstances worsened, his appearance grew raffish with a certain stylish defiance. This was the brief 1903–4 period of the white peaked cap, tennis shoes, seedy flannels, and the famous ashplant. Recklessness was not native to him. He resumed his studied neatness in his visits to Dublin in 1909 and 1912, and when I saw him next, after the First World War, the figure that then stepped from a taxi at our rendezvous on the Pont des Arts (and that I was to see whenever later occasion brought me to Paris) had grown in distinction. The adumbration of a beard tentatively came and went, the hair lay lower, the eyes that had seen and suffered so much were now obscured by powerful lenses, a cane replaced the ashplant and swung in his hand as if casually, disguising but aiding the dimmed vision; the graceful figure and carriage remained the same.

Joyce, a year older than I, had come to the College from Belvedere the year before me. I had unwisely matriculated directly after my Intermediate examination and accordingly joined him as an immature freshman in the First Arts class in 1899. He was already an established figure amongst the students, having come to the College during the Michaelmas term of 1898 to read for his matriculation and he had brought with him from his old fellow-students at Belvedere a reputation as an exceptionally gifted writer. So far as teaching can make a writer, it was at Belvedere that the neophyte learned his art. At Clongowes he was but a lad. Between Clongowes and Belvedere he was sent for a time to the O'Connell Schools, North Richmond Street, but this interlude was short.

It was from Belvedere that Joyce took all his Intermediate examinations. These exams set the standard of secondary education in Ireland, and Joyce's record was good, but not conspicuously above the average of a promising student.[1] The curriculum was a full one, distinguished from modern practice by its breadth. In his examiners' reports I have not observed any references which might be taken to bear specifically on Joyce's essay-writing—the award is what mattered—but I do quote the general criticism of Dr. Henry Evans, an exceptional examiner in English, in Joyce's last year: 'None of the compositions are exceptionally brilliant nor is any one strikingly original: but, in general, they are well thought out and expressed and containing very few cases of either faulty grammar or bad spelling. . . . Most know the figures of Rhetoric correctly.' And apropos this last sentence I cannot forbear quoting the same examiner who in the same grade in the next year examined me and surprisingly found that 'the questions in Historical Grammar with the exception of some confusion as to the use of the terms, syncope, epithesis and metathesis, have been on the whole satisfactorily answered'.

Joyce's experience with his earliest Intermediate texts left an imprint. Between 11 and 13 he was reading of Daedalus in Ovid, and of the much-enduring Ithacan in Lamb's *Adventures of Ulysses*. At that age, too, he read like all of us T. W. Lyster's *English Poetry for Young Students* and I have met none of my contemporaries who does not recall with pleasure that admirable anthology prepared by the librarian of the National Library who as such was later to be our universal counsellor and friend. It is a fair guess that it was his reading of Goldsmith in Lyster that put the schoolboy to work on his earliest set of verses, which were recovered by Padraic Colum and published by him in *Our Friend James Joyce*. Lyster, too, brought Samuel Ferguson's *Mesgedra* to the knowledge of every secondary schoolboy in the land. We knew this poem by heart: none made more use of it than Joyce. *Mesgedra* is a tale out of the Irish heroic period but Ferguson, while preserving its special character, gives it its full topographical and historical setting, so that the poem is girdled by the course of Anna Livia from where

[1] See p. 7 for details of his Intermediate marks.

The heath, the fern, the honey-fragrant furze
carpet thy cradling steeps.

until, passing the tumulus of Mesgedra's queen at Clane, near
Joyce's school at Clongowes, the

. . . limpid Liffey fresh from wood and wold,
Bridgeless and fordless, in the lonely Bay,
Sank to her rest on sands of stainless gold.

under the headland of Howth. Ferguson like Joyce beds the brown-
clear river in memories of Tristram, Isolda, and the St. Lawrences.
It is beyond conjecture that *Mesgedra* holds the seed of the most
memorable chapter of *Finnegans Wake* and also that Ferguson's
Homeric vocabulary in this poem remained in Joyce's memory.
Ferguson's epithets, the 'bard-protecting chiefs' (l. 22) and the 'ill-
befriending morn' (l. 35), plainly built up the 'bullock-befriending'
letter writer in *Ulysses* and the twice-repeated 'bullock-befriending
bard'. Maybe, too, 'the soft merchandise' of Emma's hand, yielded
to Stephen Dedalus in a round dance, owes a little to Ferguson's
'The song, the dance, the softly yielded hand' (l. 208).

These vestiges of his school reading come to light later, but his
immediate quality was quickly apparent in College in a special class
for English composition conducted by W. P. Coyne. In this class,
open to students of any year, Joyce, a newcomer, heard his essays
read as models. My friend James Murnaghan told me of one such
occasion when essays by Joyce and himself were read out as examples
of how essays should and should not be written. Exception was taken
to a sentence of Murnaghan's beginning with 'and', but this should
not be taken as evidence that Coyne was simply an academic purist.
He has some little place after Dempsey of Belvedere in the story of
Joyce's development. A pupil of Father Tom Finlay, he won a
Fellowship in the Royal, and although his real work lay in economics,
his approach to it had been through mental and moral science and he
wrote on both literature and economics in the *Lyceum* and the *Free-
man's Journal* until he left the staff of University College to join
T. P. Gill in the new Department of Agriculture and Technical
Instruction. Matthew Arnold's brother was also on the English
Faculty surviving from Newman's day. We looked into his *Manual of
English Literature* and used his Clarendon Press edition of Addison,
but apart from the interest we took in his occasional appearances and

JOYCE'S INTERMEDIATE EXAMINATION MARKS

1894 Preparatory Grade

	Latin	English*	French	Italian	Arith.	Euclid	Algebra
Max.	1,200	1,200	700	500	600	600	600
	700	455	400	211	430	230	130

1895 Junior Grade

	Latin	English*	French	Italian	Arith.	Euclid	Algebra	Natural Philosophy	Chemistry
Max.	1,200	1,200	700	500	600	600	600	500	500
	636	540	410	223	250	175	175	190	100

1896 Joyce did not enter

1897 Middle Grade

	Latin	English*	French	Commercial French	Italian	Arith.	Euclid	Algebra	Natural Philosophy
Max.	1,200	1,200	700	200	500	700	700	600	500
	642	457	528	33	342	340	180	230	175

1898 Senior Grade

	Latin	English*	French	Commercial French	Italian	Arith. and Algebra	Euclid	Trigonometry	Natural Philosophy
Max.	1,200	1,200	700	200	500	900	600	700	500
	560	650	345	102	205	145	40	20	10

* English as an examination subject included Irish and English history and geography. In each year except 1895 Joyce won a prize for English composition.

his family prestige, he enters little into the picture. In our time he took no part in the day-by-day teaching. Joyce, like myself, may have attended some of the formal public course of lectures—already mentioned—to which Tommy Arnold contributed, but our only real contact with him was at the University Orals over which, as the oldest Fellow, he presided.

The honours classes in English were taken by Father Darlington and later by Father George O'Neill, both Fellows of the Royal. As time went on Joyce's interest in these early morning classes slackened and his attendance grew more and more infrequent. For the Dean he always entertained a kindly regard and wrote to me in that strain upon his death in 1939, but to his teaching he does less than justice in *A Portrait of the Artist as a Young Man*. The Dean may have stooped to assist his pupils over academic fences invisible to Joyce; he may not have had any great capacity for continued abstract thinking; but I think none of us, including Joyce, failed to enjoy in him the quick response of a mind which went half-way out to agree with his student and to provoke and stimulate discussion from the point where agreement ended. An Englishman and a convert to Catholicism, he had an original mind, an alert, practical, and most sympathetic intelligence which made him a close friend of Gerard Manley Hopkins, but he was not, I think, really interested in literature. He was Dean of the College rather than of an English Faculty, but we all relished his unexpected sallies. While I recall his scholastic method of 'nominal and essential definitions' which left its trace on Joyce's writing, I remember better his quainter divagations in Shakespearian criticism.

But it must be confessed that the prescribed texts were not well calculated to retain the attention of a precocious student alive to contemporary literature and allergic to early hours. In their attitude to the old and new in literature, the Royal University authorities differed in no way from their fellows in the other universities in these islands. The matriculation standard was naturally not greatly higher than the final of a secondary school; the reading courses in English literature for the next two years were confined to a very limited number of texts, and the cautious approach of the degree class to the nineteenth century proceeded no further than the Romantic School. Such indispensable fodder was quickly and easily assimilated and it left, at any rate, much time for outside reading. In Joyce's case Byron, Shelley, and Newman had made a pre-collegiate lodgement;

Pater and his off-the-course reading had brought him far along paths untrodden by his fellows. As a seventeen-year-old student his interest lay in Yeats and Blake and the French Symbolists; Dante lay a couple of years ahead in the curriculum but had already joined Ibsen as one of his gods, with D'Annunzio as their somewhat incongruous thurifer. A few of his books, bought, signed, and dated by Joyce at this period, came later into my possession.[1] They are evidence of the early preoccupation with the theatre which brought him in 1899 to the first performances of the Irish Literary Theatre and in 1900 to the paper he read to the Literary and Historical Society of the College on 'Drama and Life' and his *Fortnightly Review* article on 'Ibsen's New Drama'.

This article written on *When We Dead Awaken* is the earliest published piece of Joyce's prose. Its appearance in the *Fortnightly* made something of a sensation in the College and enormously enhanced the prestige of its eighteen-year-old author. Mainly expository, by reason of its subject, it stands as the confession of the writer's admiration of the Scandinavian dramatist whose intransigent qualities he sought to make his own. Written when he was preparing his paper on 'Drama and Life', we may infer that the article contains not merely identical opinions but perhaps actual passages from the unpublished address. This is evident enough from the touching letter he wrote to Ibsen a year later when he heard that the *Fortnightly* article, coming under Ibsen's notice, had pleased the old man. In that letter Joyce referred to the College debating society where he had vindicated Ibsen's rightful position in the history of the drama and had drawn attention to his 'lofty impersonal power' as well as to his other claims. 'I have', he wrote, 'sounded your name defiantly

---

[1] D'Annunzio: *La Gloria* (Milan, 1899). Signed on the cover and fly-leaf and dated 'September 1900' by Joyce. *Sogno d'un Tramonto d'Autumno* (Milan, 1899). Signed and dated 'September 1900' by Joyce. *La Gioconda* (Milan, 1900). Signed and dated 'May 1900' by Joyce. Hauptmann: *The Coming of Peace* (London, 1900), trans. Janet Achurch and C. E. Wheeler. Signed and dated 'February 1900' by Joyce. *Hanelle, A Dream Poem* (London, n.d.), trans. William Archer. Signed on the cover and fly-leaf and dated 'August 1900' by Joyce. Ibsen: *Little Eyolf* (London, 1897), trans. William Archer. Signed and dated '1900' by Joyce. *The Wild Duck* [I cannot now trace details of this]. Maeterlinck: *Alladine and Palomides, Interior, The Death of Tintagile* (London, 1899), 1 vol., authorized translation. Signed and dated '1899' by Joyce. *Pelleas and Melisanda, The Sightless* (London, n.d.), trans. Laurence Alma Tadema. Signed and dated '1899' by Joyce. Verlaine: *Les Poètes maudits* (Paris, 1900). Initialled 'J. A. J.' and dated '1902'.

through the college where it was either unknown or known faintly and darkly.' And he continues:

But we always keep the dearest things to ourselves. I did not tell them what bound me closest to you. I did not say how what I could discern dimly of your life was my pride to see, how your battles inspired me . . . how your wilful resolution to wrest the secret from life gave me heart, and how in your absolute indifference to public canons of art, friends and shibboleths you walked in the light of your inward heroism.

Joyce had been elected to the committee of the Literary and Historical Society in 1899, and his paper 'Drama and Life' was read to the Society on 20 January 1900. In that season, 1899–1900, Arthur Clery was auditor. He was devoted to the stage. He had, indeed, made mention of Ibsen before Joyce in an address to the Society on the contemporary theatre—a few months after Joyce entered College and before any of the Irish Literary Theatre's performances. To read papers to the Society was a distinction, to take part in debates was the right of all members—and a right at times stormily exercised—but the reading of a paper was a matter of invitation rarely extended to any but the more senior. That this invitation should have been issued to Joyce in the term following the performance of *The Countess Cathleen* and before his *Fortnightly* article appeared, was a clear and friendly recognition of his minority stand and of the general desire to hear him on a subject he had made peculiarly his own.

For reasons one may only guess at, 'Drama and Life' was not published in Joyce's lifetime. Like *Stephen Hero* he may have thought it a 'schoolboy production', and a text lay dormant in his brother's diary until 1959.[1] In that long interval little of its first reading survived in the memory of those who heard it. To my regret I was not one of them, and my inquiries amongst those who were present bore little fruit. Now I set down what I learned then, although the diary text has seen the light of day. It seems to me worth while to reproduce what I have written unaltered, together with my own early speculations, if only to recapture the reactions of Joyce's first audience.

John Marcus O'Sullivan, who spoke to the paper, remembered neither the address nor even that he himself had taken any part in

---

[1] This text is in Mason and Ellman, *The Critical Writings of James Joyce* (London, 1959).

the proceedings. James Murnaghan told me that the paper began with the words 'As Paracelsus says' and passed on to some reference to the *Götterdämmerung*, whereupon he professed to finding himself without any further comprehension of its meaning. He found, to his wonder, John O'Sullivan speaking to the paper but, recovering from his surprise, assumed that John O'Sullivan, being a student of philosophy, could appropriately speak as a party to this sort of esoteric conspiracy. But Murnaghan, to my mind, is a bad judge in this matter. His orderly intelligence, disciplined in the classics, revolted from the obscure and sought—in this case vainly—to reduce difficult things to words of one syllable. In general, civilized life ended for him with the eighteenth century. When not Greek, he was Mozartian: Wagner and the moderns passed him by. He was quite unlikely to go along with Joyce in the speaker's dispraise of 'the bland blatancy of Corneille, the starchglaze of Trapassi's godliness, the Pumblechookian woodenness of Calderon'. The committee of the Literary and Historical had invited George Moore to preside at this meeting, but when Moore—an unready public speaker—declined the honour, William Magennis took the chair, as later at Joyce's paper on Mangan. He admired, he told me, both performances, but of the first occasion could only remember Joyce thanking him for his attendance. He said that it was not the first service he had rendered him, since it was he who had recommended him for his Intermediate Senior Grade prize in composition. Eugene Sheehy's account to me, brief as it is, alone gives a reasonable outline. Not yet a student of the College, but knowing Joyce at Belvedere, he went to hear his friend and he followed the paper with understanding. There may conceivably have been, he said, some abstract aesthetics, but his recollection is of a debunking of romanticism and a vindication of Ibsen and the truthful handling of reality. What left the strongest impression on his memory was what he thought a most remarkable display by Joyce in his reply to the speakers. When the speakers closed at ten o'clock he rose; he had taken no notes, but taking up the speakers (W. P. Coyne, Arthur Clery, Hugh Kennedy, James J. McDonald, and the others) one by one, he dealt with each point made against him. One of his retorts referred to Hugh Kennedy as 'sheltering under the aegis of a Greek quotation'. The medicals in the back row of the Physics Theatre applauded rapturously, and breaking up at the end he remembers Seamus Clandillon clapping Joyce on the back, saying, 'You were magnificent, Joyce, but quite mad.' Eugene Sheehy, later circuit court judge, told me this before he wrote his *May it Please the Court* which gives a lively and reliable account of Joyce's early days. I have deliberately retained his account to me as supplementing his own writing.

As I have mentioned, Arthur Clery was the auditor on this particular occasion. He appears in the text of *Stephen Hero* as Whelan, the orator of the College, and Joyce quotes him, I should think with exact truth, as confessing that he had been listening to the discourse of angels without knowing the language they spoke. To establish a special relation between Stephen and McCann, Skeffington (McCann) is introduced as the auditor of the Society. In fact, he had been the auditor three years earlier. Other happenings are brought a year forward in order to emphasize Stephen's maturity. William Magennis, the Professor of Mental and Moral Science, was, as I have said, in the chair, and not W. P. Coyne. But of more material interest is the difference in the actual subject of the paper. Though, as Eugene Sheehy says, there may have been some aesthetics in it, it is certain that the main subject was a vindication of Ibsen and his place in contemporary European drama. The whole discussion on aesthetics, the 'applied Aquinas' which occupies twelve pages of *Stephen Hero*, had, I believe, no place at all in this paper. I am satisfied of this not merely by reason of Joyce's absorption at this date with Ibsen but because the title of his address was not altered, as Stephen says it was, from 'Drama and Life' to 'Art and Life'—a change which would have been necessary if aesthetics were its main subject and also because Joyce's elaboration of his 'applied Aquinas' aesthetics was, I dare to say, a matter of later date. His monologues on this topic, begun on pages 76–80 (of the New Directions edition, 1944) before the delivery of his address, are continued later to Cranly on pages 212 and 213. These monologues were heard (but much later—from 1903 onwards) by more than one of Joyce's friends. His brother, Stanislaus, was the chief, J. F. Byrne (Cranly) was another, and I myself in the autumn of 1903 and the beginning of 1904 was a third. Their subjects, the cone-shaped image of art, its disposition into the lyric, epic, and dramatic, the definition of these kinds, the Thomist constituents of beauty, were set forth to me, as no doubt to others, succinctly and dogmatically at times and places I well remember as belonging to a period three years after his 'Drama and Life'. Cavendish Row and the slopes up Rutland Square

are indissolubly associated in my mind with such discourse—conversations they can hardly be called, their sententiousness betrays the written word. They were ideas derived from St. Thomas and extended to literature, theories which he had already set down on paper when drafting the text of *Stephen Hero* in or about 1903. They were the 'flag-practices', the trying-out on friendly ears of a book in progress. A little—his special use of the term 'literature' and the definition of beauty—appeared, somewhat earlier, in his paper on Mangan.

I was fortunate enough to be present at the reading of this paper to the Literary and Historical. It was read on the evening of 1 February 1902, a coincidence with his birthday, 2 February 1882, which, if not actually designed by him, would not have escaped his attention. The meeting was held as usual in the old Physics Theatre, a large, octagonal room lit from its end bay by tall, ogival windows against which the benches rose as in an amphitheatre, crowded in the day-time with joint classes of medical and arts students, and filled on Saturday evenings by the members of the Literary and Historical and its camp-followers. On such occasions the guest chairman, auditor, and officers of the Society had their places at the long demonstration table facing the rising tiers and the reader of the paper stood to its left. Joyce's delivery is clear in my memory. He spoke in a withdrawn, impersonal way; his clear enunciation, staccato, even metallic at times; his voice impassive and very deliberate as if coming from some cold and distant oracle. In Joyce's account of Mr. Duffy, in 'A Painful Case' (*Dubliners*), 'Sometimes he caught himself listening to the sound of his own voice. . . . he heard the strange impersonal voice which he recognized as his own, insisting on the soul's incurable loneliness.' This passage reminds me strongly of Joyce's manner both in speech and his recitatives of Yeats at the piano. The voice could be singularly musical, rising and passing away in quotation or at will into characteristic aerial harmonies. It lent itself with grace to the elaborate rhythms of the prose into whose complicated web he had so studiously woven his own meditation on the quiet city of the arts and Mangan's relation to the highest knowledge and to those 'laws which do not take holiday because men and times forget them'.

Except for a quotation from 'A Swabian Popular Song', the text was printed in full in the May 1902 issue of *St. Stephen's*, the College magazine, and it has since had a wider public. Professor Hackett, who was on the editorial staff of *St. Stephen's* at the relevant date,

has written on this topic.[1] He recalls that in order to print Joyce's
complete text printers had to change type in its closing paragraphs,
and also omit this quotation, which he believes came from this poem
'A Swabian Popular Song' and probably from the end of its first
verse. He quotes the lines in his article. Other lines like:

> They would not yield their souls the thrall
> Of gold, nor sell the glory of their lays

might, I think, also have attracted Joyce's attention. Gorman mentions that he set this poem to music. I never heard him sing it nor
heard it referred to in Dublin, but Stanislaus Joyce says that his
brother made settings for some of Mangan's as well as Yeats's
poems, when living in Glengariff Parade. This would have been in
1901 or 1902.

These later readers are in a more favourable position to debate
the paper than its first audience. That audience was not wholly
dedicated to letters and Joyce's aesthetics were obscure enough even
to those who most willingly gave themselves up to his silvery incanta-
tion. His submerged or explicit references to gods and half-gods,
Bruno, Wordsworth, Baudelaire, Shakespeare, Verlaine, Novalis,
Shelley, Whitman, Poe, Blake, Swedenborg, Dowland, Moore,
Walsh, Leopardi, Dante, Ibsen, may have had something of under-
graduate parade, but they were certainly not made in self-protection
nor, in any case, would they have provided any shield against the
philistines.

This close-packed paper, prose-poem, or manifesto, will repay
close study. It has the interest of its nominal subject but in conception and execution it is in a very high degree spiritual, self-revealing
and prophetic. It drew its central theme from a sentence or two of
Yeats and John Mitchel. Yeats wrote that Ferguson restored to our
hills and rivers their epic interest, and that the nation found in Davis
a battle-cry, as in Mangan its cry of despair.[2] In his edition of

---

[1] James Meenan (ed.), *The Centenary History of the Literary and Historical
Society, U.C.D.*, 1855–1955 (Tralee, n.d.).
[2] *Dublin University Review*, November 1886.

Mangan, Mitchel wrote: 'Like Ireland's, Mangan's gaze was ever backward with vain and feeble complaint for vanished years. . . . It was easy to perceive that his being was all drowned in the blackest despair.'

The paper owed much also to Lionel Johnson who had been writing on Mangan in 1898 and more elaborately in 1900. He found in him, as Joyce did, a drifting will too ready to dwell in the valley of the shadow, haunted by memories, keening an Ireland desolate and derelict. Also, something of it was conceived in Pater's manner of an imaginary portrait; but if a second 'Nameless One' enters by way of self-portraiture, the mask is resolutely set aside in the closing passages to disclose a serene and stronger spirit.

I hardly think any one of us students present was then aware of the parallel which existed between Joyce's father and Mangan's. In an autobiographic fragment Mangan makes frequent mention of his father's irascible temper, his recklessness, and the misery it entailed on his family. His mother bore with admirable fortitude the whims of her street-angel, house-devil of a husband who, Mangan wrote, seemed to think that all feelings 'with regard to family connections and the obligations imposed by them were totally beneath his notice. . . . As a last resource he looked to the wretched members of his family for that help which he should rather have been able to extend to them. My father and mother meant well by me but they did not understand me. They held me by chains of iron.'[1]

Mangan spoke of this deplorable parent of his as a 'boa-constrictor'. In *Finnegans Wake* (London, 1939, p. 180) Joyce wrote of his own as a 'Boer-constructor' what time Shem the Penman was still a lexical student. His first audience no doubt missed the parallel, but they did not fail to pick up his allusion to Mangan as lamenting no deeper loss to his country than the loss of plaids and interlaced ornament. This topical, now obscure, allusion pointed to Edward Martyn's *Maeve* whose exacting love required her pattern of Celtic youth to equal 'the rare and delicate perfection' of Celtic ornament. It pointed also, and more immediately, to the new evangel of national dress preached in saffron kilt and plaid to the Literary and Historical just a fortnight before by Fournier d'Albe, an assistant lecturer in physics

---

[1] D. J. O'Donoghue, *Life and Writings of Mangan* (Dublin, 1897), pp. 3,10,13, 64. For Lionel Johnson on Mangan see his Introduction to Mangan's poems in the Stopford Brooke-Rolleston *Treasury of Irish Poetry* (London, 1900) and his address to the National Literary Society in May 1898.

at the College of Science—better known to us as the inventor of the particoloured, druidical Pan-Celts.

The paper disconcerted some later speakers by ignoring the politics of '48 and Mangan's share in the movement, which they had come prepared to debate. But there was enough to prick them on to battle. Joyce's tapestry presented them with no obscure allegory: the challenges were deliberate and obvious, but they were thrown down as self-evident truths and with a seeming indifference. Remote as from Sinai, but without its cloudy tumult, the lightning stabbed. It was not enough scornfully to dismiss the *Nation* poets as departing half-gods and in the teeth of the history books to qualify Mangan, the greatest of them and the friend of John Mitchel, as 'little of a patriot'. But presented first as one whose natural habitat is in the regions of ideal beauty, Mangan becomes, in Joyce's final view, the last justification of a narrow and hysterical nationalism, the passive inheritor of a tradition of griefs and failures and empty menaces, of a sterile and treacherous order, enemy of life, which would establish upon the future an intimate and far more cruel tyranny than the past of his race had known. For Mangan, a lover of death, Caitlin ni Houlihan is a queen, but for Joyce an abject queen upon whom also death is coming. Another voice, however, the voice of the speaker, is heard singing, faintly now but not to be always so; the future is with this strong spirit who will cast down with violence the high tradition of Mangan's race, its love of sorrow and despair, one who like Dante will take to its centre the life that surrounds it and fling it abroad again amid planetary music and who like Ibsen will sing of earth's joyous fullness *det dejlige vidunderlige jordliv det gaadefulde jordliv*. These were barbed, provocatory thrusts and I recall, by reason of their incongruity, two impassioned speakers impaled by them. The first was John E. Kennedy, a callow fledgling some three months in the College, whose reading at that time had travelled not far beyond *Alice in Wonderland*. Dashing first into the fray, what he wanted to know and insisted on knowing behind all Mr. Joyce's pretentious talk was whether Mangan was a drunkard or an opium-eater. He pressed his question with all the patriotic urgency at his command. At this stage Tom Kettle—perhaps on some indication from the auditor, Bob Kinahan—thought it well to get the debate running on saner and more courteous lines, but of his complimentary speech I remember nothing. But I do remember that speaker who followed him. Louis Walsh was one of the three or four recognized spokesmen of the Gaelic League, vehement and full of fire. Outraged by Joyce's assault on our nationality and traditions he let loose in the cause of the Gaelic gospel what Tim Healy, speaking of William O'Brien, called the untameable squadrons of his irrelevant eloquence. Louis's accent belonged to the Derry border which for Doric harshness can compare only with west Cork whose speech is as stones rattling from an upturned cart. Coming so soon after Joyce's silvery utterance, Louis reminded me less of a crusader in glittering mail than of a scared hen indignantly rising to no great heights on clattering wings across the farmyard.

This paper on Mangan is not mentioned by name in the surviving fragment of *Stephen Hero*, but its material, I imagine, bulks larger than 'Drama and Life' in that composite text. Its definitions of literature and beauty have been already referred to. There is as well, as I have mentioned, the more personal reference to the poet who alone is capable of absorbing in himself the life that surrounds him and of flinging it abroad amid planetary music. And there is again the 'eloquent and arrogant peroration' (*Stephen Hero*, p. 80). Whether 'Mangan' or the earlier 'Drama and Life' was the 'first of my explosives' (*S.H.*, p. 81) is immaterial. One need not be misled by Stephen's indignation; Joyce regarded him with more ironical eyes. Was his fate, after all, so dreadful or the explosive reckoned so deadly? The fowler had spread his nets and caught the unwary. His other hearers stood free and approved the performance. How else explain the note of the meeting sent by the Society's secretary to the *Freeman's Journal* to appear in its columns on Monday 3 February? It reported categorically that it was 'the best paper ever read before the Society'. This student opinion was re-echoed in the next issue of *St. Stephen's*, which described the paper as 'reaching an unusual height of eloquence' and 'displaying exceptional qualities of thought and style'. Glancing at the two speakers I have mentioned, the same writer, William Dawson, tartly commented on 'the philistinism of young Ulster' and on 'the ignorance which had a field day for the nonce'. Furthermore, the editor and staff saw to it that the 'explosive' should have its fullest detonation at the earliest moment. Ibsen, too, in early days had written of the 'torpedoes' he had placed under the 'Ark'. Joyce's explosives echoed these. The editor printed the address in his next issue, a few months after 'The Day of the Rabblement' had been declined.

St. Stephen's, in which I, too, had a later hand, was a light-hearted students' paper with just sufficient ballast to give it weight outside College circles. Its publication coincided with the days when an old University grievance was being agitated, and many alternate schemes put forward. These were the subject of continual reference in its columns. The magazine was published within the College, and subject to ordinary college discipline; and since it was so sanctioned by the authorities and guaranteed by them against financial loss, its most casual observations might not unfairly be regarded by outsiders as evidence of more than student opinion. In those sensitive days and in hostile quarters the opinion of any contributor might easily be turned to other and not always relevant purpose. Circumstances of time and place must enter, therefore, into any judgement of its editorial conduct; and they enter here into the rejection of 'The Day of the Rabblement' and of Skeffington's article on the position of women.

Dated 15 October 1901, 'The Day of the Rabblement' was prompted by the approaching performances of the Yeats–Moore *Diarmuid and Gránia* and of Hyde's *Casadh an t-Súgáin*. It shows the young writer parting company with the Irish Literary Theatre on the issue of national drama. A short article, trenchant in criticism, imperious in manner, it is none the less, for a manifesto, occasionally oblique and allusively obscure. The relevancy of one or two passages still escapes me. I do not yet, for example, understand what precisely underlies the topical reference, 'today when the highest form of art [meaning, I suppose, drama] has been just preserved by desperate sacrifices', nor can I identify the occasion of Yeats's recent association with a platform from which even self-respect should have urged him to refrain. It certainly coincided with the moment when Yeats stood closest to the Gaelic League, when the Irish Literary Theatre was about to stage its first play in Irish, and when Yeats was writing to Lady Gregory that its organ *Beltaine* 'should be a Gaelic propaganda paper this time'. It was at this date I first heard Yeats address a meeting—at a Gaelic League *sgoruidheacht* in the Gresham Hotel. Velvet-coated, with black, flowing tie and a black lock of hair falling over his forehead, he leant forward from his great height, snapping back again like an uncoiled spring, as he told us that he looked forward to the day when his own books would be unread in an Ireland that had become Irish-speaking. We applauded the self-sacrificing gesture. Did any of all this really earn, except in one young man's eyes, the reproach of a lost self-respect?

Joyce's paper began with the now familiar reference to the Nolan —an allusion which Joyce found irresistible.[1] In the same opening sentence he takes from D'Annunzio's *Le Vergini delle Rocce* Leonardo da Vinci's epigraph concerning the necessary isolation of the artist, and in later passages he refers to both D'Annunzio and Bruno. I propose to return in a later chapter to these first traces of D'Annunzio's influence as well as to the unexpected mention of the Danish novelist, Jens Peter Jacobsen. These allusions were more than literary flourishes. In his expression of pure disillusionment, however, the ardent young student left no one in doubt as to where his quarrel with the Irish Literary Theatre lay. At the start, its promoters seemed to him allies of the contemporary European movement. Ibsen, D'Annunzio, Hauptmann, and Maeterlinck: these names with Yeats's own held for Joyce the promise of the future. *Beltaine* held out this promise; its first number began with the word 'Norway' and references to Ibsen and the new drama filled its pages. When Yeats wrote that the new Irish Theatre would do its best to give Ireland a hardy, national character by opening its door to the four winds of the world instead of leaving the east door alone open, he was setting out a programme that Joyce would have welcomed. But supplementary statements were more disquieting and the programme of the Theatre in its third year went no way towards redeeming its promise. No winds blew from Scandinavia or the Continent. Inspiration was sought only from a western province, and the impatient idealist set down in 'The Day of the Rabblement' his sense of an unworthy surrender to the popular will. Rightly or wrongly he found its root in Yeats's treacherous instinct for adaptability and in the poet's 'floating will'. His reproach seems now surprising; Joyce's hawk-eye had found, I think, this latter phrase and the threatened capitulation of the poet in one of our college texts for that year. In Corneille's *Cinna* the suspicious Émilie rebukes her lover for his *esprit flottant* and like Joyce bids him:

> *Va, sers la tyrannie*
> *Abandonne ton âme à son lâche génie.*

He would also remember that Lionel Johnson had found in Mangan a 'floating will'.

---

[1] *Spaccio della Bestia Trionfante*, registered by the Nolan, is Giordano Bruno's title to his treatise on ethics. Yeats's article 'Ireland and the Arts', written for the *United Irishman* in 1901 and republished in his *Ideas of Good and Evil* (London, 1903), sets out his position at this date.

Joyce's standpoint was too well known in the College for his protest to shock the editorial staff of *St. Stephen's*, nor had his *de haut en bas* treatment of the promoters of the Theatre anything in it to offend them. The Theatre had already been under their fire from a diametrically opposite point. They might disagree with both, but left to themselves they would, I am certain, have found the essay useful material for further controversial copy. It was, however, denied publication at the instance of the college authorities. On my very much later inquiry I was told by John Marcus O'Sullivan, a member of the editorial staff whose recollection was clear, that the rejection turned on a single point—the reference to D'Annunzio's *Il Fuoco*. This novel, with much else of D'Annunzio, stood in the Roman Index. Unreserved commendation was inconsistent with the position of the responsible head of college teaching and Joyce's article was accordingly returned to him. I never heard that there was any suggestion of its revision by the writer. That would have been a fruitless endeavour even if the editor knew then—as is known now—what D'Annunzio meant to Joyce at that stage of his growth.

The other instance of college censorship occurred later when Frank Skeffington, then the college Registrar, submitted an article on co-education in the university. Inasmuch as it was written by the Registrar it might appear to lend some semi-official authority on a point of college management. This article was also returned, whereupon both incongruously were issued together in pamphlet form.

My memory of these college years between 1899 and 1902 holds pictures which differ from Joyce's presentation of college life in *Stephen Hero* and the *Portrait of the Artist*. The divergencies do not subtract from the essential character of the central figure. Little or nothing that the writer says is without its element of truth in fact or in the poetic imagination. The space between is the no-man's-land of art, but it is always well to remember that Joyce did what he could to destroy the MS. of *Stephen Hero* and looked with 'disagreeable surprise' upon the survival and ultimate publication of its fragments. These texts have made everyone familiar with the picture of the artist–student absorbed in the aesthetics of literature, jealous of his independence, scornful of his fellows, standing on his defence, arrogantly aloof. He moves with an occasional companion against a frieze of figures, outlined with sharp realism and chosen to represent what he, using Ibsen's word, would always refer to as the 'trolls'—forces threatening his integrity. These selected figures serve the artist's purpose in accentuating his isolation and maturity. They existed in truth and in fact but they should not be accepted as the authentic background of college life nor as a film of complete actuality. After all, he himself wrote, 'It must not be supposed that the university lacked an intelligent centre.'

Joyce lived a withdrawn life. Reserve, as he said, was always a light penance to Stephen Dedalus, though Joyce's detachment was more than reserve. No artist is without egoism, but the ineradicable egoism with which he endowed Stephen was evident enough to repel or keep at a distance some—and not the least reasonable—of his class-mates. Reticence makes few friends amongst youth. Joyce had listened to Flaubert's advice, '*Fais-toi une cuirasse secrète composée de poésie et d'orgueil*,' which was D'Annunzio's also. He buttressed his instinct for self-preservation with what he called a breakwater of order built up against the sordid tides of life without and within. He schooled himself to silence, and this breakwater was rarely breached. He easily assumed a mask—that common end-of-the-century stage property—and it was rarely dropped.

Looking back, I see nothing of Stephen's 'shivering society' but young men going their ways: sometimes together, a few alone, and amongst them Joyce—peculiarly isolated. I see nowhere hostility to him except in the rough-and-tumble of debate. Joyce's furrow was narrow and deep, but there were other minds amongst his fellows quite as active as his own. I have written of some of them elsewhere. I found them, then as now, quite allergic to 'trolls'. Their beliefs were as conscientiously held as Joyce's and as freely arrived at, and no more open than his to any unworthy capitulations. They were students of philosophy, law, science, classics, and economics. Mallarmé and Rimbaud were names not wholly unknown to them, but their principal studies and interests were quite different from Joyce's preoccupations. He was self-centred and centripetal; they were, in the manner of all students, gregarious. In the college societies, on the steps of the National Library, wherever they met they plunged into debate. Night after night when the Library had closed they would continue their interminable discussions, swinging backwards and forwards between their lodgings, loath to separate, unwilling to conclude anything.

In short, they lived as all students since Abélard or Duns Scotus have lived. But Joyce stood aside from such debate; his conclusions were already arrived at, *in petto*. They recognized his distinction, accepted his aloofness from discussion, and retained his friendship or goodwill. Some of his school friends—notably Richard and Eugene Sheehy—were in this group and here there was no question of distance. With them he gave free play to his sense of the burlesque, introducing it with gravest aplomb in the most incongruous circumstances. At their hospitable house in Belvedere Place, in the good Dublin fashion of those years, the carpet would be taken up of a Sunday evening and the night went in music, dancing, and impromptus. Joyce was a very welcome visitor there and he lent himself with great gusto to the improvised charades. He travestied indifferently Ovid, Shakespeare, and street-singers. Eugene Sheehy has already, like myself, recorded his playing of the queen mother in *Hamlet*, distraught and rocking herself with grief at the sight of Willie Fallon (another of his Belvedere schoolfellows) as the mad Ophelia, strewing the floor with cauliflowers. Eugene Sheehy might also have mentioned, because he took part in it, that unusual papal conclave dated very near the beginning of the century at which Joyce, as Rampolla, instructed his aged fellow-cardinals in the proper electoral procedure, meticulously and very clearly spelling out his name to them, R-A-M-P-O-L-L-A, for their better guidance in voting. Charades had lost none of their popularity in the theatre-loving town and, indeed, for the next few years they raged from house to house. At the Morrows' house in Effra Road the half-hanging of Bulmer Hobson as General Munro, or some such Ulster United man, nearly ended in disaster, and further out at Dun Emer I have painful recollections of myself as Master Builder Solness falling down the front of the house through rose bushes and thorns past the window of the drawing-room where the audience were, while Kitty McCormack sang of harps in the air.

Joyce brought this sort of play-acting into one at least of his college classes. Abandoning his English lectures, he was a fairly regular attender at Professor Cadic's French class which was held at a not unreasonably early hour. Cadic, a Breton of no great academic distinction, was a good, conscientious, and kindly teacher who loved but imperfectly understood the fantastic ways of Irish students. At any rate he forgave them everything if their antics were conducted in French; as once, for example, when George Clancy (who later as Mayor of Limerick was murdered by the Black and Tans) sat opposite Joyce in class. Cadic knew they were good friends and was all the more surprised when Joyce, on that day, took great umbrage at some invented remark of Clancy. With great dignity Joyce elaborated a point of honour which Clancy rudely brushed aside. Joyce's punctilio sharpened. Clancy's rudeness got near the *mot de Cambronne*. Cadic vainly tried the role of peacemaker, but blood alone could wipe out the insult and the cartel was coldly drawn up by Joyce for the meeting in the Phoenix Park. The whole class had to intervene before insulted and insulter shook hands across the table and Racine or Boileau was resumed—but not however until they had solemnly in turn advanced to the head of the table to kiss on both cheeks their 'Papa Cadic'.

Cadic, if no great scholar, was a patriotic Frenchman and something of an elocutionist. Each year in his class, for the sake of some newcomer or apropos Du Guesclin or Joan of Arc, one of us would revive the memories of the *année terrible* and would seem to remember that our dear master had played an honourable though youthful part in its sad happenings. Did he not also share in the defence of the sacred soil of the *patrie*? Cadic would then admit that from all the schools in his *département* he, a child, had won the highest award for elocution, and when the war came he had been sent out by the administration to all its platforms reciting verses in aid of the war charities. Ladies tore off their bracelets and heaped jewels upon him. Could he, by chance, remember such admirable verse? Well, perhaps he could, and so Racine was again set aside while our dear Papa recited his ode once more, moving his audience to a profound emotion and to unnumbered tears.

Sometimes, again, the grateful class would be persuaded to hand up French essays. To me, essay-writing in any language, was always an odious *corveé*, a thing to be evaded; one essay in French I remember for the same reason as I remember certain passages from Joyce's paper on Mangan. By this time the class had been enlarged and was held on certain occasions in the Aula Maxima; and the theme prescribed for it had been 'Bells'. I contented myself with fabricating a pseudo-French version of Schiller's *Lied von der Glocke* and escaped worse disaster. Cadic sorrowfully passed over such attempts, but he read out Joyce's essay which seemed to me to be a piece of pure lyricism. Its musical onomatopoeia must have been remarkable to sound still in my not very retentive ears. From little country *clochers* bells tintinnabulated in Joyce's prose or solemn bourdons reverberated and died away in distant harmonies. Reborn, their echoes vibrate in his later pages.

Harmonies were innate in Joyce, and so word-catching was second nature. Ben Jonson was one of his quarries. But an early example of his interest in a new scientific vocabulary dated from his 1899–1900 Physics class. Physics, or Natural Philosophy as it was called then, was an obligatory subject in his matriculation and First Arts examinations and Joyce accordingly attended Professor Stewart's lectures in the Physics Theatre. Stewart was fond of underscoring his demonstrations with quotations from Gilbert and Sullivan. This appears in the *Portrait of the Artist*, but with it also his elliptical and ellipsoidal distinction which becomes the object of Moynihan's (i.e. Bob Kinahan's) ribaldry. More curious, perhaps, is his reference to platinoid and its recent discovery by F. W. Martino. Felix Hackett reminds me that this verbal loot of Joyce goes back to this class where we were students together. He also points out to me that Joyce mixes up the separate vocabularies appropriate to a lecture on electricity and a lecture on dynamics, which the meticulous Stewart would never have done.

Joyce, I imagine, found his Italian class the most sympathetic and rewarding of any. *Stephen Hero* represents himself as choosing Italian as an optional subject, partly to read Dante, and partly to escape the crush at French and German lectures. In fact, the degree in modern literature for which Joyce was reading required English and two foreign languages, and he had already been working at Italian and French for at least six years before entering University College. The seven or eight of us around Cadic's table at the French class made no great crush; in the German class I had Bob Kinahan as the sole companion of my first year, and later I was alone with *Faust* or *Die Braut von Messina*, or brooding, not for the last time, on the use of the Chorus in Greek tragedy. Eugene Sheehy has described Joyce in Father Ghezzi's Italian class—the pair constituted the entire class—and he complained to me that he made nothing of it because Joyce and Ghezzi spent the whole time discussing philosophy in an Italian too esoteric or too fluent for him. Yet Joyce's truly optional subjects, pursued at home or in the National Library, were Danish and German. When I, as a student, was entering into closer relations with him, he had read much of Ibsen in Danish, and he quotes Ibsen in Danish in his Mangan paper. To what extent he spoke the language I do not know, but liking to direct my attention to the poetical element in Ibsen, he would repeat verses like *Agnes, min dejlige Sommerfugl* from *Brand*. At the same time, attracted by

Hauptmann, he was interesting himself in German, translating for another exercise *Michael Kramer* and *Vor Sonnenaufgang*. All this, I should think, would be about 1902.

It is rarely possible to pinpoint the moment when friendly acquaintance, at least as between man and man, passes into friendship. But it was in the academic year 1901 that my accidental student acquaintance with Joyce was established on a more friendly footing. Up till then he was a figure whose appearance at class I looked for and relished. My friends were then, for the most part, outside my literature classes. One was a philosopher, one a physicist, the others were heading towards law and medicine. But as the curriculum grew more specialized in the degree classes, Joyce and I saw more of each other, and our reading helped to better acquaintance. Mine was routine, enlarged by the National Library and the second-hand bookshops. In this routine of the advancing years at university the procession of the English classics filed by, accompanied by their linkmen and torchboys—they also in their appropriate hierarchies and place. On the heels of Coleridge and Matthew Arnold came Bradley on Shakespearian tragedy and something of W. P. Ker, much of Saintsbury and a little, and that little too much, of Dowden; in their train followed the painstaking biographers of the *English Men of Letters*. It was still the age of the Romantics in poetry and of character-diviners in criticism. In criticism Coleridge was our closest study and made the deepest impression. He ruled the critical roost—but Saintsbury fluttered more extensively. Saintsbury bobbed up everywhere, both in French and in English. His baroque style, his zest, his blind spots, his chaotic, sometimes wrong-headed, enthusiasms, his contagious delight in a magical verse: all were attractive compared with Bradley's profundities or Dowden's idolatrous character-dowsing. My memory still fondly dwells on Saintsbury, that industrious man who fixed his professorial chair on so many perches. We met him on both our English and our French courses, 'very nearly' (as he characteristically wrote of Tom Moore), 'very nearly if not quite on the top of two trees which if not quite cedars of Lebanon are more than mere grass of Parnassus'. It was, therefore, with a peculiar pleasure I found Joyce in 1922 requesting Miss Weaver to send Saintsbury a copy of *Ulysses*, writing, 'I am old fashioned enough to admire him though he may not return the compliment. He is quite capable of flinging the tome back through your window.'

These were the critics who received corrective consideration at the hands of our Aristotelian and scholastic lecturers. Much of their class-work commentary was necessarily routine work but now and then it was stimulating. It did not occur to me then, nor does it now, that it was obscurantist or thought-repressive. On the contrary, discussion was invited and carried on à l'outrance. However, I do not recall any general treatment of aesthetics in the English class, apart from Coleridge and Aristotle. I myself had more roving aesthetic debate when reading Goethe and Schiller with George O'Neill, my German professor. His taste was narrow and more rigorous than mine, but his judgements were acute and well based. In the French class there was good linguistic teaching, but little or no literary argument. Curious, and significant of nineteenth-century taste, there was no Racine. Alongside the periwigged classics, Corneille, Molière, Boileau, Fénelon, Voltaire, we read our Lanson, Taine, the rigid Brunetière, and again Saintsbury, making what we could of these intelligent, contradictory authorities. In any case, dredge as I may in memory, I cannot find Joyce sharing in any of these critical exercises. Assiduous in Italian, he followed the French class mainly for the sake of the language, but his attendance at the English class was, I have already said, perfunctory. However, it was sufficient to leave with him an impression of Father Darlington that affected both his matter and his method. He heard more 'applied Aquinas' from him than from anyone else in those days. He appreciated his quality and, holding his memory in respect, wrote to me kindly upon the death of his well-intentioned teacher.

Lightly as was this routine of college reading observed by Joyce, its track can be followed in his early writings; 'the ragged book written by a Portuguese', which taught the young artist 'what little he knew of the laws of Latin verse', was the familiar *Prosody* by Alvarez used in our Latin class. In its Dublin edition this ingenious composition of a Portugese Jesuit who died in 1582, having been Rector of colleges in Coimbra, Evora, and Lisbon, must have been the last relic in our schools of late Renaissance, classical teaching, and one may still admire the dexterity of its Latin mnemonic lines and the accuracy and brevity of its rules. *Hamlet* belonged to our Second Arts year, 1901, with Sidney, Spenser, Bacon, and Milton; and in the same year Joyce was reading for his Italian examination Petrarch and Dante, Castiglione's *Courtier*, Leopardi, and the *Oreste* of Alfieri, which Stephen Dedalus read with Father Artifone, in its wretched Italian binding, along with 'the dingy chronicle of Machiavelli'.

Such courses are the reasonable, methodical approach to the quiet city of the arts, but students have turbulent minds not always or even ordinarily content with their conditioned serenity. We preferred the free pastures of the National Library, and what the second-hand bookshops offered. The book-barrows too, like Johnson's *Dictionary*, provided fine, confused feeding. In those days the second-hand bookshops, i.e. Webb's, Neale's, Massey's, and Clohessy's, were well stocked. Bennett's, the auctioneers on Ormond Quay, held monthly book sales and their overflow, drifting down the river, silted up on the book-carts in Aston's Row, where Pat McGrath, Clohessy, and Perdissart presided at their twopenny table d'hôte while 'Clicky' Walsh, the runner, hovered about, knowing his clients' taste and purse, ready to fetch out from his pocket a special *bonne bouche*. Pat McGrath was a dealer of quite different calibre, and I would not have his name forgotten. Lame and frail, he was a most loved personality in this Row, with a special store in his living quarters near by in Temple Bar, to which he would welcome various students. He had no mean knowledge even of eighteenth-century Irish literature.

Whither on Saturday afternoons flocked the booklovers: M'Clintock Dix, Séamus O Casaide, and D. J. O'Donoghue; our seniors, John O'Leary and Count Plunkett; an odd professor or two like Dowden, and later Osborn Bergin and H. O. White, with their generation of Arthur Griffith, Padraic Colum, Seumas O'Sullivan, Henderson of the Abbey, and O'Leary Curtis. Dowden found there Shelley's *Address to the Irish People*, and Professor Bergin and I had a long-standing, never-won, bet to equal that rare performance. The poet Seumas O'Sullivan was master in this art. He had special divination in his prehensile fingers, which led them, without looking, and without breaking off his talk, to some eighteenth-century curios. His jaunts to London were paid for by selling on one side of the Charing Cross Road what he bought on the other. On the book-carts of Aston's Row Stephen Dedalus found his dingy texts, but also *The Tables of the Law*. It was possible for the impecunious student—and there was none other—substantially to supplement his college ration.

This cheap market introduced an engaging element of chance into one's reading, and encouraged promiscuous adventure. In my own case, I was at that time reading perhaps as much in French as in English. The sober brown wrapper and clinging pages of the *Revue des deux mondes*, unchanged since the days of Buloz, were in the National Library and held for me its serials: Fogazzaro's *Il Santo* or Bourget's *L'Étape*. I could get on the carts for myself the issue of *Cosmopolis* that held Mallarmé's *Un Coup de dés jamais n'abolira le hasard*, and I can trace the beginning of one line of reading to an early purchase there of Maxime du Camp's two-volume *Souvenirs littéraires* which set me off on the Second Empire and its antecedents and led me on to Verlaine, the Parnassians, and the Symbolists. It was at this point, I imagine, that Joyce and I began to compare notes or, more precisely, it was now that Joyce found another receptive ear and an auditor who would lend him his meek attention. A year later another link was added when I was looking forward to my first journey abroad and to a fairly extensive tour in Italy. This prospect, together with my growing interest in the arts, plunged me into Italian history and my casual reading, taking a more definite direction, became wider and even more superficial. Anything that concerned Italy I read eagerly. As a schoolboy, drawn as he should be to the champions of popular liberty, I had read *Rienzi* and *Romola* and to these were early added all the Italian novels of Marion Crawford on the shelves of the municipal libraries. Now came, in international spate, the travel literature of Hare, W. D. Howells, and Maurice Hewlett; of Gautier, Taine, and Michelet; of W. W. Story, Hawthorne, and more Crawford. All these with much Pater and Ruskin, and the histories of John Addington Symonds, Sismondi, and Villari were gluttonously consumed. With more difficulty I stumbled with translation and text through Dante and a little of the courtly poets and more of Leopardi and Carducci, and borne on by a newborn Franciscan enthusiasm, I one day landed up via Ozanam's *Poètes franciscains en Italie au XIIIe siècle* on Jacopone da Todi. The stranger figure of Joachim di Flora and of the apocryphal *Eternal Gospel* I had come on by way of history as Joyce had by way of Yeats's *Tables of the Law*.

Amongst my new contacts with Joyce I remember particularly Jacopone and Dante. Joyce was probably amused at my flounderings in those Elysian fields and bog-lands, and I was glad to seize on any lifelines he threw out. I might add the name of a third writer to whom at this time I was devoted: Huysmans's *œuvre* was as familiar to me as to Joyce. His *La Cathédrale* was before the public for two or three years and his survey of religious art and symbolism was read at the time by anyone who, like Edward Martyn, was interested in liturgical reform and was not unduly shocked by the violence of Huysmans's attack on *bondieuserie*. When Joyce came back from Paris in 1903 he wrote him down as an obvious comedian, who had wearied his audience, and as a writer without form. But whatever he may have thought of Durtal's spiritual pilgrimage or of Huysmans's elaboration of a schematic, recondite symbolism, I think Huysmans entered a little way into the writing both of *Stephen Hero* and the *Portrait of the Artist*, if it was no more than by his manner of dogmatic, professorial exposition.

Huysmans's symbolism of colours fitted in, too, with the Rimbaud sonnet, *Voyelles*, which Joyce would repeat to me. Imitating Rimbaud and *A Rebours*, we would push these *fin-de-siècle* fancies, as I imagine students were doing in every university town, to the correspondence of colours with the sounds of musical instruments and with the sense of taste, compiling, for example, monochrome meals, tables d'hôte in black puddings and caviare, black sole with Guinness and black coffee. But if he did repeat Rimbaud's sonnet it was not because he was given to reciting verse. Unlike the other young writers of my experience he had not the habit of speaking his own verse or rapturously reciting Yeats or Swinburne or Verlaine. Singing was his release and, unlike other students, his talk was not of his reading. For the rest of us literature was largely matter for criticism, an affair of contrasts and tendencies. For Joyce it had absolute value, it was a world of integral beauty.

So far, therefore, as I recall them, his references to books were fragmentary and only by way of illustration or—most often—by way of reference to something in which I myself was interested. Ibsen, the truth-compeller, the heroic intransigent, was by this time above controversy. At no time did I hear Joyce discuss him as a social reformer—such propaganda was to him inadmissible—and he was first to direct me away from such journalistic criticism to the poetry and symbolism of *Peer Gynt*, *Brand*, and *The Master Builder*. Flaubert frequently cropped up in our talk; it was Joyce who made me read *La Légende de Saint Julien l'Hospitalier*, that ingenious piece of literary *vitrail*, most probably because he was aware of my interest in stained glass and knew from my reading of Huysmans that I was as keen to see the church of St. Séverin in Paris as I was to see Notre-Dame. But he himself, as an apprentice craftsman, was more interested in the fatuous doings of Bouvard and Pecuchet, in Flaubert's collection of 'cases', and in what Elizabeth Bowen calls 'the exquisite compilation of a *cliché* dictionary for additions to which one strained one's ears at gatherings'. He was already collecting 'epiphanies'. Of the French poets I can remember him quoting much from Verlaine and something of Baudelaire, de Nerval, and Hérédia, but nothing except an odd line from Mallarmé, and nothing except the sonnet from Rimbaud whose work, though it is diametrically opposed in its origin, in certain other ways has a curious resemblance to Joyce's writing.

Amongst English writers, Pater—the deep-freeze of so much end-of-the-century prose—was studied by all budding stylists, but George Meredith was more widely read and discussed. Prejudiced in his favour by his liberal sentiments, we students were not deterred by his quick plunges from the spring-board of fact into fancy. We took his mannered allusiveness and headlong cataracts of imagery and simile in good part and as a challenge. The introductory chapter of *Diana of the Crossways* was accepted as the touchstone of an emancipated intelligence. I still look with some amusement at my copies of *The Egoist* and *The Tragi-Comedians* of which one belonged to Frank Skeffington and where almost every line is underscored or marked by his impulsive, exclamatory pencil. Pater, I am pretty sure, had followed the 'silver-veined' Newman in Joyce's pre-Ibsen school-days and may have taught him to poise an adverb. He lifted his eyebrows when I said I found Meredith in *Stephen Hero*. When I suggested that some of the sentences in that MS. were as involved and obscure as Meredith's own, he wondered at my obtuseness. Joyce's opinion of Meredith at this time appears in his review of Douglas Jerrold's study in the *English Men of Letters* series:

No one can deny to Mr. Meredith an occasional power of direct compelling speech . . .[but he is lacking in] the lyrical impulse, which, it seems, has been often taken from the wise and given unto the foolish. . . . These novels have, for the part most, no value as epical art. . . . But they have a distinct value as philosophical essays . . .[1]

Of Henry James, who was new to me, he spoke admiringly, and in connexion with the same draft of *Stephen Hero* turned me to *The Portrait of a Lady*.

One need not attach more significance to such names occurring in casual talk than their circumstances warrant. None of them had anything like the importance that Ibsen, D'Annunzio, Blake, and Yeats had for Joyce at this time. Yeats's verse we all knew, admired, and recited, but Joyce's admiration was less limited and extended to

[1] *Daily Express* (Dublin), 11 December 1902.

The Tables of the Law and *The Adoration of the Magi*—tales which left most of us cold. Their apparatus of magic seemed to us flimsy tools for one who sought to restore Irish letters, and to be but the distillation of the magic which aureoled and bedevilled Yeats's early path before the artist sloughed off artifice and stood out in his own light. Joyce praised these inventions to me in terms I found hard to reconcile with his stronger admiration for Ibsen's uncompromising search for truth in the conflict of 'average lives'. He found in them, no doubt, as in Blake and Maeterlinck, the breaking up of a 'sterile and treacherous order' and the same perception of 'far-reaching conflicts independent of his actors' that he found in Ibsen's drama. The influence of Arthur Symons was hardly less. He was then playing a part in criticism comparable with Ezra Pound's in later years and he influenced writers greater than himself—amongst them Joyce, to whom he was encouragingly kind. His *Symbolist Movement in Literature* (published in 1899) was dedicated to W. B. Yeats. It introduced most of us to the movement abroad. It was ardently read and it supplied much ammunition to *Beltaine* and *Samhain* and the manifestoes of the Irish Literary Theatre. A single quotation from it fairly represents both his own point of view and the direction of Joyce's mind:

Symbolism . . . comes to us now . . . offering us the only escape from our many imprisonments. . . . And it is on the lines of that spiritualizing of the word, that perfecting of form in its capacity for allusion and suggestion, that confidence in the eternal correspondence between the visible and the invisible universe . . . that literature must now prove, it if is in any sense to move forward.

Whether thanks to Symons or not, Joyce had acquaintance with Baudelaire, Verlaine, and the Symbolists in his earliest college years. He was talking of them, anyway, in 1900, and his copy of Verlaine's *Les Poètes maudits* is dated 1902 by him. He may have bought it in Dublin or during his first visit to Paris in that year, but it may, just as well, represent an older interest in these poets—Rimbaud, Mallarmé, Villiers de l'Isle Adam, and Verlaine himself—of whose writings it is an anthology with comments. It contains Rimbaud's *Le Bâteau ivre* as well as his *Voyelles* and that other sonnet *Oraison du soir*, 'savamment et froidement outre', as Verlaine qualifies it, for which Joyce furnishes cold and equally deliberate parallels.

Verlaine was a special favourite of his, but to find an immediate influence of these other Symbolists on Joyce's work would be to anticipate many years' experiment. To ignore it at any time is more unreasonable. '*Que veut dire symbolisme*,' asks Remy de Gourmont, '. . . *anti-naturalisme . . . tendance à ne prendre dans la vie que le détail characteristique, à ne prêter attention qu'à l'acte par lequel un homme se distingue d'un autre homme.*' Does not this point again to the 'epiphanies'? Correspondences, beginning with those that were the subject of Baudelaire's sonnet, always fascinated Joyce and riveted his attention and when Baudelaire speaks of *confuses paroles*

> *Comme de longs échos qui de loin se confondent*
> *Dans une ténébreuse et profonde unité,*
> *Vaste comme la nuit et comme la clarté.*

he is not only bridging the space between Romantics and Symbolists by way of Mallarmé and Rimbaud but he is also pointing towards Joyce's last experiments. Rimbaud's verbal alchemy and Mallarmé's use of words 'that take light from mutual reflection' remaking 'out of many vocables . . . an entire word, new, unknown to the language . . .' are at no great remove from *Finnegans Wake*. Baudelaire may hold our attention a moment longer to recall him in *Le Cygne* crossing Paris, his memory invaded with thoughts of a Trojan river which in its poor cracked mirror reflects the sorrows of the exiled Andromache. And the poet sees in his path a swan dragging its fair plumage in the city mud, convulsively lifting neck and head as it strains like Daedalus, *l'homme d'Ovide*, to the ironic skies as if reproaching God.

Like symbolism, theosophy was in the air in the nineties. As a schoolboy reading W. T. Stead's *Review of Reviews* in my father's house I was dimly aware of the ambiguous figure of Madame Blavatsky. Later, in the pages of the *Lyceum* (the early University College publication), I read more of the cloudy origins of theosophy and its hierophants and heard something of the Hermetic Society, which, grouped about A.E., existed for some time in Dublin as a theosophic centre until, wearied of schisms and charlatans, it settled down as a discussion group attentive to A.E. In early days at the National Library I ran across A. P. Sinnett's *Esoteric Buddhism* but neither it nor its Irish echoes made any lodgement in my hospitable mind. Joyce also had turned over its pages and, if I was repelled by the condescendingly pretentious claims of theosophy and in general by the pantheist's surrender of free will, I cannot imagine that Joyce was much more seriously influenced, even though its vocabulary enters a little into his early writing. What Père Maréchal calls its refusal to recognize the sovereign liberty of the creative act would be sufficient in the long run to repel Joyce.

Tom Kettle excepted, Joyce was the first of my University College intimates to make the acquaintance of A.E. and W. B. Yeats. His seeking out of the two poets recalls the youthful Rimbaud's quest for his two *voyants*. Years afterwards, A.E. told me of that first meeting and I set down his account of it from a note I made at that time. It is an oft-told story—Yeats had written his side of it and Stanislaus Joyce another—but I give it as A.E. told it to me. The meeting, I imagine, would have been in 1902. A.E. said that one night, on arriving home to his house in Coulson Avenue about half past eleven, a good-looking young man called on him and asked him if he was Mr. George Russell. The youth apologized for calling at so late an hour and said he had been waiting for an hour and a half at the corner of the street for his return. A.E. brought him into his room and sat with his legs curled up under him, a pipe hanging from the side of his mouth, while Joyce explained that he had a difficulty in stating precisely what he wished to speak to him of. A.E. said he would do the talking until the reason emerged. But after some time and after another inquiry Joyce was still reluctant to speak. A.E. said he would then have to proceed in Socratic fashion and said that like Gaul he was divided into three parts: economics, poetry, and painting. Had Mr. Joyce called to discuss anything connected with economics? Joyce emphatically said 'No'. They came to poetry, and Joyce admitted he was seeking a new avatar and had hoped to find him in A.E. but on seeing him he had instantly made up his mind that he was not the man.

They spoke of Yeats and after some praise Joyce said that Yeats had now gone over to the rabble. When he left, A.E. wrote to Yeats that what he had long threatened him with had come true; that the new generation was knocking at the door. Joyce afterwards called on Yeats who reported back to A.E. that when he had praised some of Joyce's poems Joyce said he cared no more for his criticism than for that of the man in the street. Joyce said, 'What does it matter? In a little time, both of us, perhaps, will be forgotten.' Yeats entered on a subtle and elaborate defence of his development to the effect that while a young man might exclusively dedicate himself to beauty and consider that alone, he may, as he progresses, devote himself with propriety to experiment. Joyce flew out at this as showing how Yeats had deteriorated and finally he left the room with a parting shot: 'I

come too late to influence you; you are too old.' Neither Yeats nor A.E.
would be averse to shaping a tale to an effective climax, but for as
long as I knew him Joyce invariably spoke in the most friendly and
respectful terms of Yeats, and I am still unwilling to accept these
words as *ipsissima verba*. Joyce was uniformly courteous and to those
he disliked or who disappointed him he was coldly formal. It is
inconceivable to me that as a young man he would have waited upon
his senior, sought his opinion unasked on his verses, and then turned
him and his criticism down in such arrogant terms.

A good deal has been said of Joyce's youthful arrogance. Some
things that he admired and most things that he rejected were admired
or rejected by him in the teeth of his fellows. He was curt or, if you
wish, arrogant, in the defiant proclamation or defence of these opinions. He was not so in behaviour or social conduct. He was aloof,
wary, dogmatic in statement, and mistrustful. He was scornful of the
opposition he anticipated and he was peremptory in his reply. To
that extent, and to that extent only, he was arrogant. Youthful shy-
ness, self-consciousness, arrogance, pose or enigmatic mask—one
may interminably debate these points for what they are and draw
supporting arguments from his writing without very definite con-
clusion. One may draw *post scriptum* argument from Rimbaud but
get no further than to find the characteristic expression at a certain
stage of a certain type of mind. Stephen Dedalus confesses to throw-
ing up defence works in the busy construction of the enigma of a
manner. That enigmatic manner was very evident in Joyce in these
student years.

Rickword has written of the precocious Rimbaud as arrogant,
diffident, timid, perverse, self-conscious, incapable of that momen-
tary surrender of one's egoism necessary to social intercourse.
Another critic has written

True, there is something enigmatic about [Rimbaud's] *persona* . . . something in the last resort aloof, something never entirely communicated. This
oracular quality is mysterious and therefore confusing. But, as with all
such temperaments, with all persons whom we call *reserved*, the mystery
lies less in the substance than in the manner.[1]

This latter quotation seems to me exactly appropriate to the present
instance and indeed corresponds with what I have written. But it
need not be carried further. Neither Joyce's early self-consciousness

[1] *T.L.S.*, 9 October 1953.

nor his undeniable egoism were serious barriers to social intercourse. Even when most marked they would break down in a gust of sudden laughter and occasionally, in congenial company, in sustained bouts of hilarious drollery.

Joyce was not naturally a good 'mixer', but he was not anti-social. He was difficult but not uncompaniable. At no time, then or in later years, do I remember him in company taking part in any general discussion. For anything approaching serious talk he preferred the company of one to many, and even then you had to meet him on his own ground. You were reduced to the docile recipient of his earlier meditation, sententiously delivered. Many found his trick of recondite allusion affected. He certainly used it to evade reply. He did not debate. Question was turned aside by dark or gnomic answer. He himself said he offered the gift of certitude and loved the enigmatic. But to the healthy-minded student the proffer of certitude is a challenge and the unriddling of enigmas a pastime. It was the doubling of these parts which gave his speech an air of arrogance and it made for isolation in the student body, but not hostility. It faded out on closer acquaintance and indeed wholly disappeared in later years. But the cryptic answer, the reticence on deep issues, which always seemed to me his dominant characteristic, never disappeared. He was ready enough to enter into explanation of his attitude towards many things, but irony, wry humour, grotesquerie, courteous evasion, or silence—each in turn was enlisted to build up an impregnable defence against intrusion on the inner sanctuary. *Ibo singulariter donec transeam.*

Compared with the rest of us Joyce's reading was unusual. A great share of our reading was, as I have suggested, extra-curricular but it was on the whole bent towards our college studies. Joyce's was directed to his own single purpose. His familiarity with contemporary European literature was greater than that any of us could pretend to—again with the exception of Tom Kettle. He read Blake closely in the Ellis–Yeats edition. As a word-catcher, but not as a word-catcher only, he studied the Elizabethans and Jacobeans. His reading was selective and purposeful and, far from being that dangerous animal, *homo unius libri*, he chewed the cud of his favourites rather than devoured many. He was diligent in following up clues and the modish allusions to more esoteric writers in Yeats and the French Symbolists. His extraordinary memory and natural acuteness did the rest in the way of preserving for use immediately,

or after a great space of years, what came his way. So far as I could
see, between 1899 and 1904 he was not a notably assiduous reader in
the National Library, but his reading hours may well have been my
class hours. He was, of course, an *habitué* and had his favourite
table; it was his base, a sort of poste restante, but he was not nailed
to it: he did not keep regular hours as those of us who did three-hour
seances. It may have been otherwise with him at the Bibliothèque
Ste Geneviève in the winter of 1902, but in the years I speak of he
seemed to me to spend rather less time in the National Library than
in roaming, again like Rimbaud, 'with hypnotized steps through the
streets of his little town, his *beaux yeux d'azur noyés dans l'extase*'.
Neither did he frequent the book-barrows, though we met there
occasionally. His circumstances did not permit him to accumulate
many books, but if he was neither bookworm nor borrower nor book-
collector he was quick to claim his property when he found it and he
knew where to look for it. He says as much in the *Portrait of the
Artist*: 'The lore which he was believed to pass his days brooding
upon . . . was only a garner of slender sentences from Aristotle's
Poetics and psychology' and a synopsis of St. Thomas.

Balzac wrote three novels out of a summary of Swedenborg,
winning thereby some credit as a mystic. It would not be just to say
that Joyce's scholasticism had as insecure a foundation. It would be
untrue, for the natural bent of his mind was towards the realism of
Aristotle and Aquinas, but this does not imply that amount of recondite reading which some commentators, to whom the tradition
of scholarship is unknown, attribute to him. To these anything that
touches the medieval is strange, wonderful, and smacks of murky
superstition. Though Joyce's attendance at the English classes in
University College was infrequent, the garner of slender sentences
to which he refers is the same harvesting of Aristotelian definitions
which his class-mates meekly gathered into their own memory or
notebooks from Father Darlington's lectures. As to Aquinas, I must
also mention Boedder's *Natural Theology*, the textbook used in
the class of religious doctrine open to all students. He had a page or
two on Thomistic aesthetics starting out with *pulchra enim dicuntur
ea quae visa placent*. Rickaby's *General Metaphysics* was read in the
philosophy classes. Joyce could not but have seen it in the hands of
his friends who were reading philosophy including, for example,
J. F. Byrne (Cranly), who sat at the same table with him in the
National Library and at least in the first week of the term would

have opened its pages. Rickaby, between pages 148 and 151, holds the marrow of Joyce's aesthetics. It is Rickaby who quotes from St. Thomas well nigh all that Joyce uses touching the good and the beautiful which by its mere contemplation sets the appetite at rest. He discusses its unity, or *integritas*, its harmony of parts or, *consonantia*, and its clear lustre, or *claritas*; commonplaces, it may be said. But for me an intriguing detail is that Rickaby illustrates part of his argument by a sudden unlikely reference to a barn, just as Joyce, in his talk with Lynch, suddenly invokes the basket on the head of a passing butcher's boy.

These Stoneyhurst manuals would have escaped the attention of no intelligent student in the College; Joyce could have got what he wanted from them in half an hour. He could as easily have garnered further fodder from the two or three pages of De Wulf's *Introduction à la philosophie néo-scholastique*, in which one finds a clear enough outline of the plan utilized by Joyce's 'applied Aquinas'. There, as in the other textbooks I have mentioned, he would have found the enjoyment of aesthetic pleasure to reside formally in disinterested contemplation and its perception to be of the intellectual order. He would have found not merely Aquinas's three requisites for beauty, ending with the radiant *'resplendentia formae'*, but also more than the seed of Joyce's 'epiphanies'. The *claritas pulchri* on which Stephen Dedalus broods is defined as having in view that 'property of things in virtue of which the objective elements of their beauty—order, harmony, proportion—reveal themselves clearly to the intelligence and so elicit its prolonged easy contemplation'. Joyce's epiphanies have a wider range, but their source lies between Aquinas and Flaubert.[1]

Whatever, for a season, his reading may have been in the Bibliothèque Ste Geneviève, Joyce did not follow any of the philosophy courses in University College, and there is no record of his attendance at any meeting of the Academy of St. Thomas, a discussion group meeting irregularly to read papers and debate (mainly from a neo-scholastic standpoint) any philosophic theme. Such papers, in Joyce's period, ranged from Epictetus to Bacon and the neo-Kantians. His acquaintance with St. Thomas derived, I am satisfied, not from such meetings and certainly not from any formal study of

---

[1] My quotations are from Dr. Coffey's translation published in 1907, but De Wulf's *Introduction* was published in 1904 and it incorporates material from his earlier studies in the aesthetics of St. Thomas published in 1896.

philosophy, scholastic or otherwise, in the College. It would have begun in the sodality and advanced classes for religious instruction in Belvedere. A similar sodality and class were open to all students in University College; their general instruction followed the scholastic pattern, and the authorites read or cited were, as I have said, lying at hand about the College. But the same principles, *ad mentem divi S. Thomae*, his vocabulary and definitions made part of the general atmosphere of college discussions and entered into basic criticism in the literature classes. Joyce had much the same experience of it in English and Italian as I had in German and English. Speaking for myself, a great deal of my German reading was accompanied by the friendliest wrangles across the table with my professor, with whom I occasionally agreed, and in which Aristotle, Aquinas, Baumgarten, and Scherer were the acolytes of Lessing, Schiller, and Goethe. Joyce's scholastic definitions are sprinkled through some reviews he was writing for the *Daily Express* in the winter of 1902; later I was listening to them in monologues on aesthetics which remain in my memory as much from the manner of their exposition as from the matter. The dry, staccato delivery of these *pronunciamientos* was appropriate to their scholasticism, and their didactic certitude squared with the hard core of his mind. What held my attention then was the seeming difference between their sharp concreteness and his devotion to Ibsen and the Symbolists and, in particular, to Verlaine and Yeats: Verlaine strongly influenced the verse he was writing at this time. But our talks were rarely on this aesthetic level; they went with casual meetings as we crossed town together to the north side and ran mostly on the theatre or music, and chance topics.

It seems curious to me now, when I think of Joyce's perambulations of the city and our later absorbing interest in everything that pertained to it, that nothing of its history or aspect cropped up in our conversation. It is not fair to say that the visual arts at no time existed for Joyce. He recognized their existence and their right to prevail with other people, whose interest in them he watched with friendly eyes. But at no time did he seem to me to take a disinterested pleasure in painting, sculpture, or architecture. The growing infirmity of his sight would explain this indifference in his later years, but the same unawareness seemed to me to exist in his early years when his eyesight, though weak, was not yet gravely impaired. There were family portraits in his father's house, which after many vicissi-

tudes hung in his own Paris apartment side by side with later portraits, and with two of Jack Yeats's canvases—one of the Liffey at
Leixlip, the other showing the river with one of Guinness's barges.
He cared for these for their associations. He took a polite interest in
the work of his painter acquaintances and in the protean changes
which art underwent in the new century, but he showed no youthful
inclination of his own in these directions. All my student friends
were devoted to the theatre; some of them shared an equal interest
in painting or music. But I never once saw Joyce in the National
Gallery or at any picture exhibition or heard him make any comment
on Dublin painting or architecture. In the matter of painting I can
however, recall one slight instance. Before any of his work had been
seen in Dublin, I entertained from reproductions a liking for Puvis de
Chavannes. I must have mentioned him to Joyce, who surprised me
a little later by praising his touching *Pauvre Pêcheur*, which I did not
know. Joyce was at pains to fetch me out a volume on Puvis in the
National Library to show me its reproduction. I had spoken of his
murals in the Panthéon and Sorbonne and when Joyce returned in
the spring of 1903 after a six months stay in Paris I asked him what
he thought of them. He passed the Panthéon, I suppose, every day
in that six months, yet he had never gone in to see them. The incident
is trivial but it betrays a certain indifference to painting, and shows
still more the characteristic interest he took in his friends' tastes.

Similarly in regard to architecture. He knew the streets of Dublin
by heart and his memory was a map of the town. But his interest in
its buildings, as in pictures, was for their associations. On this point
I have the advantage of a note kindly given me by Mr. J. J. O'Neill,
a former Librarian of University College, who, at the period with
which I deal, was a member of T. W. Lyster's staff in the National
Library and had for a colleague Mr. Seán T. O'Kelly, later to be the
distinguished President of Ireland. I transcribe the note as follows:

My outstanding recollection of James Joyce is meeting him in the Capel
Street Municipal Library in company with Seán T. O'Kelly on the occasion
of a lecture by John Kells Ingram. Lyster was in the chair and I clearly remember Ingram advising his audience to read the newspapers that were
opposed to their political beliefs, as this would lead to the working man
thinking for himself and not blindly following the programme of the
politicians. After the lecture, Joyce, Seán T. and myself walked along
Britain Street (now Parnell Street) and when we arrived at the junction of
Dominick Street I pointed out the house where Leonard McNally lived.

Joyce did not show much interest in McNally as a political personage but when I mentioned he was also a dramatist and had written one poem that had attained a certain popularity, he enquired the name of the poem, and when told it was 'The Lass of Richmond Hill' Joyce said 'Richmond Hill, that is in Rathmines'. I said, 'as far as I know it is not the Richmond Hill in Dublin or London but it is a place in Yorkshire.' Joyce seemed disappointed and said he would look it up. A few days later, I met him in Molesworth Street and he informed me I was correct in my location of McNally's poem. Later after the lecture I showed Joyce Sir Samuel Ferguson's house in North Great George's Street and Parnell's House in Temple Street. He appeared much interested and spoke for a considerable time on both Ferguson and Parnell.

In those days there was a Dublin antiquary named Edward Evans, author of a formidable little work entitled *Dublin Almanacs and Directories*. He also occasionally contributed articles of historical interest to the *Irish Builder*. Evans and I became very friendly and we frequently took walks in the evenings through the city streets when he would point out houses that had been at one time the residences of celebrated literary and historic characters. Indeed it was from this source that I laid the foundation of my knowledge of old Dublin which afterwards I was able to pass on to another Irish writer, W. J. Lawrence, the historian of the Irish stage.

Joyce in those days lived in St. Peter's road, Cabra, and was frequently seen in the company of Oliver Gogarty. I met them one autumn night and walked up the Cabra Road, listening to Joyce and Gogarty discussing Shelley. I think that Dowden's *Life* was the book they had in mind. Curiously enough, that afternoon I heard Lyster praise an essay on Shelley that had been published by the Browning Society and Joyce said he would like to read the essay. (It was wholly like Lyster that he should also have forced this essay on my attention when reading in the Library.) A few days later I gave him the book in the Library. Joyce told me to continue my study of the topography and history of Dublin as I appeared to have gained a large amount of information on the subject. I showed him Lady Morgan's house in Kildare Street and the Emmet house in Molesworth Street on another occasion.

This was in 1904, years before the Georgian Society began its study of Dublin architecture and before our eighteenth century became a fashion. But it is none the less singular that, in one who so assiduously paced the stones of Dublin, so little of its most characteristic aspect enters into his writing. Its life was an unfailing stimulus, its skies and the furniture of its streets reflected his mood but the graceful untenanted shell gave him no special pleasure.

Music, on the other hand, was an abiding passion. It was a heritage from both sides of his family. His mother as well as his father was a singer, and also a pianist. It may be because his home was at this time so full of song that to his regret he neglected any formal study of music. He was content to play the piano by ear and, except for a few singing lessons, made no other systematic study. A group of us, college friends, went regularly to the orchestral concerts which Esposito established and maintained over all this decade, to our inestimable gain. Joyce went to none of these. Singing and the opera sufficed for him and he could spend an indefinite time singing at the piano bending with uplifted hands over the keyboard. So I remember him at the piano in the Aula Maxima of the College on a day which marked a stage in our growing intimacy, as it was then that he told me of the death of his younger brother, George, to whom he was deeply attached, and whom his family and teachers regarded as of equal literary promise with himself. He was fifteen when he died. Joyce sang to me two of Yeats's songs, 'Who Will Go Drive With Fergus Now' and Aleel's song from *The Countess Cathleen*, 'Impetuous Heart, Be Still, Be Still', to which he had set music of his own. His brother had asked him to sing them to him as, in his last illness, he lay in an adjoining room. Yeats's 'Had I the Heavens' Embroidered Cloths' was another song to which he had at this time put music. All three he sang in simple recitative modulated with a few supporting chords, singing or chanting in the manner of Florence Farr with her psaltery whom Yeats had introduced to our stage. Others, new to me, were written by Henry VIII and Queen Elizabeth: 'Pastime with Good Company', 'I Love and Shall Until I Die', and 'Ah, the Sighs that Come from the Heart', songs which he probably found in Hullah's *Miscellany*, and the old ballad 'Turpin Hero'. Some of these he would sing on Sunday evenings at the Sheehys' with a variety of others, which I set down as I remember: Yeats's 'Down by the Salley Gardens', 'When First I Saw Your Face', 'Spanish Ladies', 'The Croppy Boy', 'I Arise from Dreams of Thee', 'The Man that Broke the Bank at Monte Carlo', 'Blarney Castle', 'When McCarthy Took the Flure at Enniscorthy', and 'Molly I Can't Say You're Honest'. His sisters recalled to me another, their favourite—'In Her Simplicity'. Rightly or wrongly they laughingly spoke of a sad ballad, 'The Lass of Aughrim', which, they said, Joyce was perpetually singing at home.[1] He purported to know thirty-five verses of it but they could recall only a few lines:

[1] But see Mr. Donagh MacDonagh's article in *Hibernia*, June 1967.

> The rain falls on my heavy hair
> And the dew wets my skin,
> If you be the Lord Gregory
> Open and let me in.

A dialogue proceeds with the man's

> What was my last gift to you?

and the girl's reply:

> My babe lies cold in my arms,
> Lord Gregory, let me in.

These are a few of the songs out of his great and varied store—some of his own acquiring, more coming from the inexhaustible stock which was his father's, but all very much part of himself. Not many that I heard him sing at that date were from Italian opera. There was Balfe or an odd Gounod or Arthur Sullivan. That may possibly have been because he did not want to obtrude Italian upon his audience. At any rate, his familiarity with Italian opera, through his father's knowledge of it, was nothing like the extensive knowledge that his later residence abroad brought him. But at that time his acquaintance with the Dublin music-hall and with the repertoire of the entertainers who ran one-man shows was prodigious. I find in letters passing between us in 1937 that his interest in Ashcroft, Wheatley, Val Vousden the elder, Percy French, and their peers was still unquenched, and that I could ransack the music shops for them and the *libretti* of old Dublin pantomimes without satiating it. This appetite was independent of their special value to him as raw material. His father had a quite exceptional familiarity with all this vernacular undergrowth of song as well as an old love for the Italian opera. In the 1900s, Mozart and Balfe excepted, Wagner was beginning to oust the older school from our stage. One rarely heard of Donizetti, Bellini, and Rossini, except on the concert platforms. But they lived on in the memory of the older generation and Joyce had knowledge of the singers through his father, whom in other letters he mentioned to me as listening with his friend, James Gunn, one of the two proprietors of the Gaiety, at the back of the darkened theatre when Tietjens and Trebelli were rehearsing.

His early singing, as I remember it, was that of a light tenor, exact and pure in pitch and tone, and particularly notable for its clear articulation. He held the words in equal respect with the music.

But absorbed as he was in literature, it never then entered my mind that he entertained the possibility of a career as a singer nor indeed would I have thought that the volume of his voice, then practically untrained, would have allowed it.

Up to 1902 I knew little or nothing of Joyce's family circumstances or of his financial conditions, which were then becoming ever more straitened. Many of us students were living with our families and in my case a monthly allowance that could be reckoned in shillings was ample to provide me with tram fare, theatre and concert entertainment, and additions to my growing library. My friends may have been in better or worse case. Those who lived in lodgings diligently compared with each other the value they got from their landladies. Otherwise I do not remember any talk of money. We lived alike as poor students, very conscious of our high status as such, but we seemed to do all we wanted to do with no iron necessity compelling us to the contrary. Our futures lay before us, not very closely considered but on the whole clearly enough outlined. Without any thought on the matter I assumed that it was not otherwise with Joyce. His ambitions and his capacity lay obviously in literature. Whether they were to be fulfilled by solitary effort or through journalism never came up for discussion. But in October 1902, when we both took our degree, it was plain enough that Joyce was at a loose end and in difficult circumstances. His determination to live for letters was no less and he surprised us by entering his name as a student of the Medical School in Cecilia Street. He told me in all seeming seriousness that he proposed to make a fortune as a doctor in a few years in order to devote the rest of his life to literature. I could hardly imagine him giving such extended credit to the medieval tag, *dat Galenus opes*, yet when with equal abruptness he left Dublin immediately afterwards he presented himself in Paris at the Collège de Médecine, as if the first step was in deliberate preparation for the second. I cannot conceive either to be other than his first desperate resolve to be quit of his domestic entanglements and to live, however precariously, free from otherwise inescapable burdens.

Recalled after six months of great hardship by his mother's fatal illness, he turned to singing as to teaching for his bare support. Both were temporary expedients only. If he had meditated music as his profession, a serious artist like himself would have taken up its study with complete thoroughness. As it was, he counted amongst his friends a half-dozen who had easy access to the concert platform and so he made it a temporary objective. The usual preliminary, then as now, was to win distinction at the Feis Ceoil. Joyce had, as I recall it, one or two exploratory interviews with Signor Palmieri of the Irish Academy of Music. Palmieri was himself a Feis prize-winner in that year, 1904, for his oratorio, *The Exodus*, with a libretto by Thomas MacDonagh. He approached Joyce, but after the event, with an unaccepted offer of training based on a percentage of his future earnings. In fact it was Vincent O'Brien, Count John McCormack's first singing master and lifelong friend, who did all he could to prepare him for the competition. The test pieces were the recitative, 'Whom God Loveth He Chastiseth', and the aria, 'Come Ye Children' (from Sir Arthur Sullivan), an Irish air by Moffatt, 'A Long Farewell', and a short sight-reading test. Vincent O'Brien found himself with an unusual pupil and sorrowfully lamented to me that Joyce's discussion of the message conveyed in the recitative took largely from the time which should have been given to music. I was present at the competition in May at the Antient Concert Rooms. Joyce sang the recitative and aria magnificently, and in voice and artistry was clearly superior to his rivals. But, the sight-reading test being handed to him, he studied it for a moment and then laid it down on the piano and abruptly left the platform. Accordingly, he missed the gold medal. My wife, who was then unknown to me, was also present. She knew Joyce only by appearance but not quite as he appeared on this occasion—an angelic chorister in a butterfly tie and the whitest of linen. An old lady behind her exclaimed, 'Oh, what a nice boy', and shared our general disappointment when Joyce's failure to attempt the sight-reading test debarred him from the highest award. Luigi Denza, famous as the composer of 'Funiculi, Funicula', was the adjudicator, and in his report to the Feis Ceoil Committee it was significant that he made no reference to the first or second prize-winner, but added, 'I would recommend the tenor who obtained the bronze medal to persevere in studying seriously.' John McCormack had won the gold medal in the preceding year. Eugene Sheehy told me that, as youngsters, Joyce and one of his brothers amused themselves occasionally by singing outside houses on the Howth Road. It was a pastime not unknown to others. The lovable Eugene Collins, a witty raconteur, fine singer, and able solicitor, played pranks of that sort in his early days, with a banjo at English holiday resorts, but he folded up when he spotted an Irish judge in his audience. My wife similarly told that once, being asked to a party at George Moore's, she put a shawl over her party frock, and sang ballads of her own collection outside his house in Ely Place. It was in the early days of the folk-song fashion. George hated itinerant musicians, but she sang touchingly, and a friend within recognized the then unfamiliar air, 'I Know My Love', and sent George down to give the singer her sixpence. Helen returned it to him when she appeared a little later in the drawing-room without her shawl.

Not all Joyce's concert engagements were much more remunerative, useful though they were to him at that time. The programme of one concert where he appears with some of his friends to whom I have alluded, can still be seen. Others were more like the one which Joseph Holloway mentions in his diary, less profitable in sterling than to literature. The concert was supposed to be in aid of our Irish industrial movement and was held in the Antient Concert Rooms. Holloway tartly comments on its slack management and its noisy stewards. Eileen Reidy, the accompanist, left early—for good reason; her improvised substitute proved incompetent. Joyce was one of the irritated company of artists and, when his accompanist broke down, he sat down himself at the piano, and strummed his own accompaniment to 'In Her Simplicity' and 'The Croppy Boy'. Out of these tears 'A Mother' in *Dubliners* was born.

A few brief notes from me to Joyce, dating from this period, survive in the Cornell University Library, and have only recently come under my notice. They had faded from my memory apart from the circumstances of their origin, and I read them now after half a century not so much for their intrinsic interest, which is only personal, as wondering at their odyssey from Dublin to Trieste and to Ithaca, N.Y., and as illustrating how tenacious Joyce was of any trifle that touched his affairs. The first dates from the weeks before the Dublin Feis Ceoil of 1904, and relates to collections of Irish airs made by Patrick Weston Joyce, M.R.I.A., one of them including some translations from the Irish by Mangan. One I was apparently lending or giving to Joyce. The note runs:

Four Courts, Dublin.

Friday May 1904.

I am sorry I was so long in locating your musical namesake but hope I am not too late. I will be around the bookshops on the Quays tomorrow about 1.30 if you chance to be there. Else I will see you in the Antient Concert Rooms next week.

C.P.C

Gimme something for *St. Stephen's.*

The next followed immediately upon the Feis competition:

My dear Joyce,
   I know you deserve a good scolding most, but failing that I don't know whether to offer you my congratulations or sympathy. It is simply scandalous that you let the first prize be thrown away, for your singing particularly of the oratorio business was throat, chest and head above the rest of the rabblement. I hope the inclusion in the list will mean that you sing at the concert on Saturday night, to take your place of honour as Dublin's Prime Platform Favourite. . .

A third—dated July 1904—removes any misconception that might derive from an article by Oliver Gogarty in *Intimations* (1950). It concerns a piano hired for Joyce's musical training.

My dear Joyce,   11.7.04.
   Herewith enclosed you will find Apollo's hire, and will pardon on its reception my clumsiness and delay in sending it on. Don't let its acceptance stand between you and your sleep of nights. It will cost me no more than a little self-restraint in passing bookshops. This is in all honesty.
Sincerely yours,
C. Curran

The fourth of these Cornell letters has nothing to do with music and its circumstances had passed completely from my recollection. It relates to some early draft of 'The Holy Office' sent me in answer to my demands for copy for *St. Stephen's*, which I was then editing. An adjective in the first sentence gives the clue and I am now, sixty years after, tickled and exhilarated at finding myself so spontaneously and peremptorily rejecting the proposed contribution. It has, at any rate, some interest in showing that both parties to the transaction took the rejection lightly to heart. The letter runs:

6, Cumberland Place, N.C.R.
8.8.4.

My dear Joyce,
   You were very safe in granting me the freedom of the press for the appended unholy thing. I feel quite imperial in my enthusiastic rejection of it. Even if the finances of the paper could stand the strain of a libel

action, the inevitable rhymes are too unpleasant for a family magazine—
so *transeat ad inferos.*

But I must have something—say, the same from a merely literary point
of view or some satirical Limericks or anything unmarketable from any
reason but one, that you have by you.

Sincerely yours,

C. Curran

I had long wondered why Joyce had never sent me his 'Holy
Office' upon his departure for Pola. He had been at pains to have
copies delivered to many of my acquaintances, the undeserving
targets of his verse. I am now satisfied that it was a courteous omission. He knew I had read it without satisfaction. I may add that my
use of the word 'imperial' is a repetition of a nickname he used
add to my christian name: Constantine. The fifth and last of these
Cornell letters, dated 1917, finds its place on a later page.

2

Later Days in Dublin

JOYCE had returned from Paris in the spring of 1903. His mother's death in the following August was a calamity, leading very shortly to the breaking-up of the family. The summer of 1904 was a struggle to keep body and soul together with a little teaching, a little reviewing, and the occasional publication of a poem or a story. It was then I read a considerable part of the text of *Stephen Hero*. The pages he had already written came to me in a bulky wad of manuscript in June 1904. Other parts he gave me in separate sections as he wrote them and before he left Dublin that autumn with the unfinished work. I had not long before entered the service of the Supreme Court, and was living in my father's house a little higher up on the North Circular Road from where Joyce had been living at Cabra. But Joyce's house, at 7 St. Peter's Terrace, Cabra, was presently sold, and Joyce went to live on the other side of the town in lodgings at 60 Shelbourne Road and for a few weeks in the Martello Tower at Sandycove. I can date the arrival of the first section from his covering letter to me, which is amongst the few of that date which have survived.

[No address]

Dear Curran,

The Accountant-General would not like me at present—black eye, sprained wrist, sprained ankle, cut chin, cut hand. I enclose eloquent note from 'Saturday Review'. For one role at least I seem unfit—that of man of honour. However, I will not groan through the post. Here is the marvellous novel delivered upon you by my twenty-third sister. An amiable creditor waited on me at breakfast yesterday for the return of fourpence which he had 'lent' me. If you are too busy to read the novel now, no harm. But as soon as you have read it send me word to meet you on some altitude where we can utter our souls unmolested. The 'Titania' people

paid me in nods and becks and wreathed smiles. The Celbridge concert
fell through. Nok sagt!

Yours heroically,

23 June 1904   Stephen Daedalus.

The next instalment came, I believe, in July and was announced
in the following manner:

The Rain,
Friday.

Dear Curran,
    Invaluable: A thousand feudal thanks: I have finished the awful
chapter—102 pages—and Russell [A. E.] has the book now. I shall send
you the chapter in a week. I am writing a series of epicteti—ten—for a
paper. I have written one. I call the series 'Dubliners' to betray the soul
of that hemiplegia or paralysis which many consider a city. Look out for
an edition de luxe of all my limericks instantly. More anon.

S.D.

We met here and there to discuss his MS.; sometimes our
rendezvous was at the North Bull. We now met there occasionally,
joined by Frank Skeffington who cut singular figures in the water,
and by Vincent O'Brien, a powerful swimmer, who once passed almost
out of our sight in the westering sun, making a lonely trek to the
North Wall lighthouse. Most often we met in some café, Bewley's
in Westmoreland Street was our favourite, but I recall no higher
'altitude' than Blacquiere Bridge over the Royal Canal at Phibsboro'
where once I found him waiting, stretched along the parapet in the
pose of the Elgin Marbles Theseus, with no other resemblance to
the Greek than appears in the photograph I took of him at that time
in the garden of our house. This photograph may well have been
taken that particular day.

I greatly regret that, notwithstanding these meetings, my recollection of the text of *Stephen Hero* is imprecise and largely unhelpful.
It is to me all the more surprising because its reading revealed to me
for the first time in any clear or connected fashion the spiritual
strain which Joyce was enduring and the sordid circumstances into
which his life had, for the moment, passed. Our earlier talks, as I
have attempted to show, had been the not exceptional converse of
students who cared about literature. By reason of his own reserve,
by reason also of my own lack, not of sympathy but of divination,
and certainly from my own reluctance to force confidences, I had
little idea of the true extent and harshness of the situation which was

hidden under his wry humour. The reading of his manuscript was therefore an experience as painful as it was engrossing. Much of our earlier talk was, I am now satisfied, in the nature of the 'flag-practices' on his friends that he has himself described. I think his loan to me of the MS. was otherwise and that it was almost as much by way of an *apologia pro vita sua* as an experiment in criticism. He knew perfectly well that I was wholly removed from his standpoint on religious matters, and that we differed equally on other issues which were vehemently agitated in the Dublin of our day. He knew also that, case-hardened though I was in letters, I was certain to be shocked at the manner of his more intimate avowals or accounts such as that of Isobel's death. Debate over such areas was accepted as futile and I was content to take the loan as a mark of friendship with a very minor role as critic or script-reader attached. This makes it all the more difficult for me to understand how little I can recall of the details of the text or where it began and ended. Memory, Sir Edward Coke said, is *infida et labilis*. My regret, however, is the less acute and my literary conscience the more lightly burdened since we know that Joyce regarded the work as a schoolboy production and, as he thought, destroyed it.

My visual memory of the MS. is of a clearly written script with remarkably few corrections or interlineations. The pages were, I would say, of the same size as my autograph copies of two poems from *Chamber Music*, that is to say $9\frac{1}{4} \times 7\frac{1}{4}$ in., but had I not seen the photostat reproductions in Professor Theodore Spencer's edition I should have thought of them as holding a few more lines. At any rate, the text was neat and easily legible and, since I had no reason to assume it was a fair copy, it was evidence of a fluent and definitive transfer of the writer's thoughts to his page. This does not imply that he had not made separate fragmentary notations of moods, ideas, and persons, which he wove into his writing. He did; that was his habit, and I think the manner of this in-weaving contributes some obscurity here and there to the comparatively apprentice writing.

I believe I read all the text written before he left Dublin in 1904, but my recollection of it is insecure. It is an untrustworthy composite doubly and trebly overlaid with my acquaintance with familiar places and people and later talk about them, with my knowledge of happenings as they actually occurred, and with the recurrence of episodes in the *Portrait of the Artist*, where they are more abruptly and sharply delineated. Some image or characterization sticks in my mind to indicate a lost passage. The North Bull episode in the *Portrait of the Artist* was certainly in one section I read, treated with the same imagery of cloud and water, and closing with the figure of the girl gazing out to sea. Such another chapter-ending was 'interminable wastes of bogland, interminable servitude of mind'; I disputed the servitude. It points me to another lost passage describing a journey through the Irish midlands—perhaps to Mullingar—when Stephen looks out from the railway carriage upon a dreary landscape, telegraph wires along the line rising and falling. I can recall also a correction I made in a topographical slip which placed Smithfield east and not west of Church Street. This points to the now missing chapter where Stephen goes to confession in the Capuchin Church. The visit is casually alluded to later in the existing text: 'The church of the Capuchins whither he had once carried the disgraceful burden of his sins' (*Stephen Hero*, p. 177). In passing, I may mention that the author, whether deliberately or not, did not remove the confusion he makes on the same page between the convent of the Capuchins in Church Street and the Franciscan library on Merchants Quay. I was reading at that time in that unfrequented library, not indeed the writings of Joachim di Flora, but the Wadding Papers.

Such fragments dredged from the past are not very helpful, nor can I hope that my more general recollections of the impression then made on me by the reading of the MS. are of any more consequence. They are evidence not so much of the real character of the text as of my own reactions at the moment. It seemed to me then anything but a schoolboy production—rather, a mature work; it impressed me by its formidable, sustained effort, its mass, its copious detail, and by the quality of the writing. At the same time it made difficult reading. There were long and involved sentences and paragraphs with elaborate rhythms and deliberate cadences—rhythms and cadences which I admired in themselves and as reflecting the writer's moods. When I repeated them, he heard the repetition with pleasure; still there was much in them that was quite obscure. These obscurities possibly occurred most frequently in early pages with their reveries on distant happenings. That is again mere conjecture, but these are the kind of passages I have in mind:

It was not part of his life to undertake an extensive alteration of society but he felt the need to express himself such an urgent need, such a real need, that he was determined no conventions of a society, however plausibly mingling pity with its tyranny, should be allowed to stand in his way, and

though a taste for elegance and detail unfitted him for the part of dema-
gogue, from his general attitude he might have been supposed not unjustly
an ally of the collectivist politicians, who are often very seriously up-
braided by opponents who believe in Jehovahs, and decalogues and judg-
ments with sacrificing the reality to an abstraction.

How could he be guilty of such foolishness, of such cynical subordination
of the actual to the abstract, if he honestly believed that an institution is to
be accounted valuable in proportion to its nearness to some actual human
need or energy and that the epithet 'vivisective' should be applied to the modern spirit as distinguished from the ancient or category-burdened spirit.[1]

It seems to me there were many such overloaded sentences which
held up an already slow-moving narrative, and this slow motion
permitted much accumulation of detail. I have already said that I
found myself thinking of George Meredith when reading the MS.
This was not, of course, that I saw anything in his writing of Meredith's glitter or his fantastic wit. But Meredith stood to us in those
days as the wholly novel example of the intellectual novelist into
whose introspective and riddling story-telling one had to mine for
treasure. Meredith's stylized obscurity, his *boutades* at the expense of
the English character and the conventions of English society, and
what long afterwards I have seen characterized in him as 'oracular
allusiveness' all seemed to me to have some equivalent in what I was
reading of Joyce. Anyway, Joyce did not seem to think so, and it was
then he mentioned Henry James's *Portrait of a Lady* where indeed
there is some resemblance to Joyce's endeavour to render, though
with less detachment, an inner life in conflict with circumstance. I
found much hard going in his involution of the inner and outer
action—if action is the right word—and James has not escaped the
same charge of obscurity.

In mentioning Henry James I do not suggest that Joyce regarded
him as his model but rather that, if anyone had to be dragged in, he
would think him a stronger candidate than Meredith and a writer at
least equally worth his consideration. If literary influences are to be
sought out, I am now much more ready to be persuaded that in these
years D'Annunzio played a greater part than is generally recognized.
Stanislaus Joyce said this clearly enough in his article in *Letteratura*
(Florence, 1941),[2] where he also shows his brother, in Trieste, a

[1] *Stephen Hero*, pp. 147 and 204.
[2] Translated into English as *Recollections of James Joyce* (New York, 1950).

lonely defender of D'Annunzio's right to use his own life and the lives of those around him as material for his art without regard to private feeling or public opinion. When Joyce was writing in Dublin I knew nothing of his attraction to D'Annunzio beyond his reference to *Il Fuoco* in 'The Day of the Rabblement' and the fact that he had been to see Duse in a D'Annunzio repertoire in London; myself, I knew little or nothing of D'Annunzio at first hand and what I knew repelled me. But the early influence of *Le Vergini delle Rocce* now seems to me unquestionable—as I hope to set out on a later page. It affected his general attitude more than his style. But, even now, on reading it I am impressed with certain resemblances between it and my memory of *Stephen Hero*: its elaboration of trailing sentences, its learned allusiveness, its alliance of landscape and figure, its diffused lyricism, its deeply felt sensuous impressions, the preoccupied apartness of the central character, and what Henry James distinguishes as its rare notations of excited sensibility. Arthur Symons describes D'Annunzio's novels as states of mind and *Le Vergini delle Rocce* in particular as a shadowy poem in which ghosts wander as if seen in a great mirror, their souls wasted away by dreams. This corresponds in some measure to the moods of reverie I recall in *Stephen Hero*, but *Stephen Hero* was a progression through states of mind and reaction from circumstance while Claudio in *Le Vergini delle Rocce* revolves about a static, half-symbolical situation. Stylistic resemblances exist. They do not touch, for example, the method of Joyce's realism. There is nothing in D'Annunzio's dialogue, sparse and sudden though it be, that essentially resembles Joyce's abrupt transitions into passages of realistic, caricatural interchange. One may dally at other points with faint surmise—on the recurrence, for example, of certain metaphors and motifs: water and the whirring of hawks' wings or the contrast between the monstrous landscapes of rocky Corace and the flat, interminable bog-lands seen by Stephen. To such speculation there is no end, but I shall return later to the more significant resemblances between the discourses which make the prelude to D'Annunzio's novel and Joyce's manifestoes.

I do not appear to have been alone at this time in finding some of the MS. obscure. John Eglinton has put on record his own opinion of the MS., arrived at when Joyce offered it or part of it for publication in *Dana*. 'Joyce observed me silently as I read and when I handed it back to him with the timid observation that I did not care to publish what was to myself incomprehensible he replaced it silently in his pocket.'[1] Stanislaus Joyce mentions a similar rejection of a shorter MS. by Fred Ryan, the assistant editor of *Dana*. I do not know whether this offer refers to the whole MS. as it then existed or to some epitome or episode—Joyce later called it an introductory chapter—or whether indeed incomprehension was his only ground for refusal. I can imagine many acceptable reasons for the editor of even this aggressive magazine of independent thought declining the whole or a part. But assuredly, if it was the whole MS. as I knew it, the author could not have replaced it in his pocket. I still think, however, that any obscurity was only occasional and would yield easily to revision. There was certainly nothing obscure in a section I read one summer's afternoon on a Dublin hillside to three or four of my intimates who were also Joyce's fellow-students. It was the account of his interview with the President of the College in regard to Ibsen and 'Drama and Life'.[2] My friends listened eagerly to the narrative, appreciated its characterization and all its points, but they wondered if such narrowly localized matter could interest a larger public.

Conspicuous in a few passages of the MS. were the coldly deliberate transgressions of 'the limits of decency' to which Joyce refers in the surviving text and the recurring tirades and railings against Church, State, and nation and the other 'trolls' who were spreading the nets of convention about the feet of the aspiring artist. These manifestoes had the effect, as I have said, of interrupting the slow course of his narrative, but I did not read them with any great concern for their literary effect. I read them, as I read the more painful account of his domestic circumstances, with interest as a personal revelation. As objective criticism of the Ireland of 1904 they seemed to me to have little validity. They were quite divorced from the Ireland I knew; they were contrary to my own experience and based on trivial or imagined occurrences. Yeats had already in 1899 written of the intellectual excitement which followed the lull in political life after the Parnell split and of premonitions of things about to happen. When Joyce was writing in 1903–4 these things were in fact happening and all sorts of converging lines were carrying from disparate,

---

[1] John Eglinton, *Irish Literary Portraits* (London, 1935).

[2] I may note that the interview with Father Delany took place much later than McCann-Skeffington's auditorship of the Literary and Historical and was not in the College garden but in the President's room and that the President did with characteristic care and courtesy accept, read, and return the Ibsen plays which Joyce lent him after the interview.

newly tapped sources unsuspected energies which in that very decade founded a new school in literature and in the next established a new State. Nothing seemed to me more inept than to qualify the focus of this activity as a hemiplegia or paralysis, however much one might quarrel with its exuberances or fanaticisms. That Joyce thought fit to call it so is the measure of his ardour and youthful impatience. But any discussion with him of such arbitrary assertions was futile; denial or attempted rebuttal was met only with some oblique, humorous, unanswerable retort. The poet was his own lawgiver, jealous and imperious, and had given his allegiance to an ideal which had nothing to do with forms of government. As Stephen Hero 'he acknowledged to himself in honest egoism that he could not take to heart the distress of a nation, the soul of which was antipathetic to his own, so bitterly as the indignity of a bad line of verse. . . . He wished to express his nature freely and fully for the benefit of a society which he would enrich.' Now his other allegiances to family and religion were deeper and already pledged. For sufficiently intelligible reasons his 'independence of soul could brook very few subjections' to the first. But it seemed to me that to forsake Catholicism for some merely apprehended invasion of his conscience, or even for some feared circumscription of his literary integrity, was strangely precipitate. In 1904 we were much more accustomed to see these tragic conflicts of faith turn on issues of rationalism or modernism. Stephen Hero's fever-fit of revolt had succeeded the fever-fit of holiness and Joyce as Stephen Hero 'desired for himself the life of an artist . . . he feared that the Church would obstruct his desire'. In this 'mood of indignation', which Joyce himself finds 'not guiltless of a certain superficiality', Stephen found Catholicism to stand in the way of full and free self-expression and 'forthwith he removed it' (*Stephen Hero*, pp. 111, 146–7, 204).

Repudiating the claims of family and country, Stephen also repudiates the Church and any discipline that might fetter his imperious will 'to walk nobly on the surface of the earth, to express oneself without pretence, to acknowledge one's own humanity'. All this—so far as it reflected Joyce's attitude—seemed to me, as I have said, precipitate, a burning of bridges before one came to them, but

> . . . mind has mountains; cliffs of fall
> Frightful, sheer, no-man-fathomed. Hold them cheap
> May who ne'er hung there.

I did not hold them cheap, but my relations with Joyce were not close enough to warrant more than sympathy, and I am not aware that anyone at any time found him willing to open up his mind on the fundamental issues involved.

It was Stephen's confessional exposures that held my first attention in the MS. and then his harsh characterization, not stopping short of caricature, of our college life and acquaintances. Humour or comic drive was notably absent. There were escapes from bitterness into reverie but the narrative remained deadly serious. Hectic ardours and emotions were recollected not in tranquillity but with morose delectation, such being the icy temper to which the writer had schooled himself to master his *Sturm und Drang*. Equally characteristic were the abrupt transitions into realistic dialogue, spatchcocked into the passages of reverie or aesthetics. That these dialogues, as has been suggested, took up a larger proportion of *Stephen Hero* than of the *Portrait of the Artist*, I am not prepared to admit. This is not my recollection. I found the introspective passages difficult and the prevailing gloom monotonous and oppressive. Under this weight the sudden voices from without came, as I remember them, as a relief in a cloudy narrative, denser I think in the early pages where the mood of recollection would naturally be most dominant. These spurts of realistic dialogue contributed an immediacy to the writing which never ceased to be poignantly intimate and they carried conviction by reason of their abruptness. The sudden shifting of planes is more evident in the finished *Portrait of the Artist* and more dexterously contrived—being, indeed, its most obvious technical device.

A friend of mine from those days found, one wet night, a drunken man lying in the roadway, and, as a Good Samaritan, he took him to the safety of the sidewalk and asked him where he lived. 'I live in the Poddle', said the drunk (the Poddle being one of Dublin's underground rivers). 'You can't live in the Poddle', my friend protested; 'the Poddle's a river.' 'I live in the Poddle', the drunk insisted, 'I live in the Poddle. It's not history we're talking.' Neither is *Stephen Hero* history. But there is enough actuality in the setting of this self-portrait of a young man 'affronting his destiny' to make misreading easy and commentators have been so misled.

Prosper Merimée called art *une déformation à propos*. In *Stephen Hero* time is, in general, foreshortened, events are telescoped, and characters are distorted or brought into a relationship momentarily and historically incorrect. The purpose is simple: to concentrate the theme in order to isolate the hero and to exaggerate—superfluously —his maturity. When he came to reconsider his early text, Joyce was himself aware of inappropriate distortion, something that needed more than the rearrangement of his material. His revision is not a matter of compression—though he was faced with the task of pruning an autobiographical novel which, half-way towards completion, had already extended to 150,000 words. In the ferment of his 'schoolboy production' we must paradoxically recognize its cold savour and also the ebullition of what the author himself, writing in the fell clutch of circumstance, had sufficient detachment to acknowledge as 'ingenuous arrogance' and 'the affectation of more brutality than was in his nature'. He can mock at Stephen's fine words, fine oaths. With similar admissions in his later text, his fellow-students may well refuse to accept Stephen's picture of college life as having anything more than a very partial, subjective validity. For this refusal, must they stand rebuked as being merely 'solicitous to cherish in every way and to advance in person the honour of Alma Mater'. Is not their own honour also engaged?

How then does Stephen's picture of University College compare with prosaic reality? Not otherwise than his picture of his home. The atmosphere is already heavy with decay, heavy with threats to his integrity. Bodeful, it is filled with stale odours of authority and decrepitude. The very houses drip. Like the young Flaubert he has 'tout jeune un pressentiment complet de la vie. C'était comme une odeur de cuisine nauséabonde qui s'échappe par un soupirail. On n'a pas besoin d'en avoir mangé pour savoir qu'elle est à faire vomir.' And, as he finds a north-side, eighteenth-century street 'the very incarnation of Irish paralysis', so at the outset we find the College, even in its external appearance, forced to conform to his worst apprehension. The building is gloomy and throws an anticipatory shadow over Stephen's mind as he crosses the Green. Not for him to take any pleasure in the contrast afforded by the eighteenth-century elegance of Clanwilliam House and its pavilion-like grace with the more sober, stately façade of John Whaley's lion-crowned construction and the transition of both by way of Hungerford Pollen's Byzantinish chapel to its pleasant residential neighbour where, in rooms overlooking the Green or with views of the mountains, most of our classes were held. Stephen, 'dim of sight and shy of spirit', did not see the stucco mythologies of No. 85, their garlands and swags upheld by playful *putti*, and the Muses led by Apollo in No. 86, the vine tendrils clustering in the Bursar's office, and the myriad birds circling on the ceilings or clamorously resounding with the fiddles and hunting horns on the walls of the grand staircase. Nothing of this, but only 'above him and beneath him and around him in little dark, dusty rooms . . . young men were engaged in the pursuit of learning'. Learning's very clothes are seedy: Alfieri is wretched, Machiavelli dingy, Alvarez ragged. And what of these young men of whom I was one and of their 'oppressive life' passed in this 'sombre building'? We were, it would appear, 'a shivering society', 'a company of decrepit youths', a day-school of terrorized boys banded together in a complicity of diffidence, eyes only for their future jobs; to secure these they will write themselves in and out of convictions, toil and labour to insinuate themselves into the good graces of the Jesuits—in common with the other inhabitants of the island entrusting their wills and minds to others that they may ensure for themselves a life of spiritual paralysis. Little wonder if the deadly chill of such an atmosphere should paralyse Stephen's heart.

I find all this insubstantial:

> This bodiless creation ecstasy
> is very cunning . . .

Confronted by this frieze of stooges against which Stephen plays his part as suffering protagonist, I find myself bewildered. I search my memory in vain for these pathetic figures, devoid of intellectual curiosity, not merely docile but servile. An odd chronic medical, a few fanatics, if you like, but not this sad company afflicted with hemiplegia of the will. To my more artless understanding the College presented itself as a single intelligent commonalty split like the atom with a variety of energies, all fascinating. Its virtue, as I have said, lay in its small numbers. Apart from the busy First Medicals there were hardly more than 150 of us in the Arts classes. We passed with healthy appetites from the academic table d'hôte to our own à la carte. Outside class this small company could split up and re-form itself into, someone has reckoned, no fewer than thirty societies. These societies had an active nucleus in students resident in the College. In their working we were all a stage army where the privates in one formation were officers in another. The Literary and Historical was the largest of them and the most vociferously representative; the smaller groupings as accurately and more tranquilly reflected our student interests. They ranged through philosophy, science, languages, music, and athletics. Papers were read and discussed by the specialists but most of us drifted carelessly from one to another, irrespective of our special studies. One, the Library Conference, was like the Literary and Historical another free-for-all, with students from every faculty joining in; the argument might concern itself with the existence of God or Shakespeare or N-rays. The Library Conference was a sort of *viva voce* book-reviewing to which anyone might introduce at his choice any new—or, for that matter, old—publication. My own contribution was Montgomery Carmichael's queer *Life of John William Walsh*. It started me on two diverging lines—Joseph de Maistre and Franciscan literature—pullulating later on my shelves to dozens of volumes. Of one thing about them all I am sure: every man spoke his own mind freely. Indeed, it would be hard to conceive otherwise with men present like Kettle or Skeffington, Felix Hackett or John Marcus O'Sullivan, or others whom I have not mentioned, like John O'Byrne or James Creed Meredith who passed from the Aquinas Society to play a public part in the revolutionary movement. They met again as judges of the Supreme Court and I do not recollect any intervention of theirs in these student debates less pungent or unshackled than their later pronouncements from the Bench.

Joyce took little or no part in such societies although they make the normal life of any university. Apart from his two addresses to the Literary and Historical he spoke but rarely at its meetings. He was present once or twice at the Aquinas or Library Conference but I think these attendances were out of courtesy to a friend. He took no interest whatsoever in the doings of the Choral Union and this was not surprising—its nineteenth-century repertory was not consonant with his idea of music, but he did occasionally make use of its piano for some gentle improvising and like most of the students he entered his name on the sodality roll, but in his first year only.

Aware as I am of this student life from which he abstained, I find it surprising that even in a cancelled work he should see in it stagnation and worse. Even as a *déformation à propos* Stephen's ecstasy in this respect appears to me as something less than cunning and his creation wholly bodiless. He is discussing fustian with his own shadow. Yeats, as I have said, showed more insight and greater detachment in a letter written to the *Daily Chronicle* in January 1899. He wrote: 'The lull in the political life of Ireland has been followed among the few by an intellectual excitement . . . and among the many by that strong sense of something about to happen which has always in all countries given the few their opportunity.' That excitement, let me repeat, ran through every fibre in the College. Such also, I think was John Eglinton's opinion. That devout student of letters, the friend of George Moore, episcopophagous rather than obscurantist, cannot be accused of undue partiality or blind solicitude for any Alma Mater. He was at that time assistant librarian in the National Library and had us daily under shrewd observation. When he came to write of Joyce in his *Irish Literary Portraits*, he introduced him as 'one of a group of lively, eager-minded young men in University College who were interested in everything new in literature and philosophy [and] in this respect far surpassed the students of Trinity College'. This seems no less than the truth.

Still less do I find these young men a servile company contentedly living under an authoritarian régime. One may accept with some reserves the picture of docile youths, mildly bent over their notebooks, patiently recording their professors' definitions. Docile, and why not? Did they not come to be taught? And who more than Joyce used his notebook and his professors' definitions to greater advantage? But, outside class, Stephen's description of a general subservience is grotesquely unreal. I have known no institution of its kind where authority was so lightly exercised. There were, to be sure, examinations to be passed. But for students like Joyce or myself there was obligatory attendance at nothing; no chores; whatever was done was done voluntarily. Professors and students worked on cordial terms and in an unforced relationship. Authority in the College, as I knew it, ran no risk of being corrupted by subservience and I do not think that many students went far out of their way in the interests of their future jobs, as Stephen says, to insinuate themselves into the good graces of the authorities. This cant of Stephen Hero is later and more appropriately placed in the *Portrait of the Artist* in the mouth of Mr. Simon Dedalus, professedly an expert in such things.

On an earlier page I have alluded to University politics as it affected college life. The matter has some relevance here in this point of subservience and I mention two incidents of these years. The first was a demonstration against the University Senate in which the President of the College was an outstanding figure. This 'Organ Row' was a characteristic ebullition of student feeling against the playing of the English anthem at our conferring of degrees. The affair, I may say, ended in the resignation of the Chancellor of the University and in the permanent discredit of the Senate. To avoid further commotion on that afternoon and to dissociate college authority from the action of the students, the President barred the students from the premises and their further demonstration was held about the college steps. It was followed, some nights later, by a students' meeting in an upper room of an old house in Middle Abbey Street over the printing plant of the newly founded Sinn Fein. The place was lit by flaring gas-jets and candles. The room was packed out with students crowded on top of each other, standing on window-ledges, and hanging from window and door cases. Young barristers like Tom Kettle had come down from the Law Library, and with them the brilliant and short-lived John O'Mahony who was to advise us on the legal steps to be taken against the plainly illegal action of the Senate who had, at their formal meeting, gone grievously wrong in a point of fact. For the first time I heard familiar reference to mandamus and quo warranto, this time from the lips of Hugh MacNeill, a professor of Latin at the College, the Professor McHugh of *Ulysses*. The meeting was gusty, deadly serious, tumultuous, and yet orderly. With Carlyle in my mind I saw myself at the Club of the Jacobins with the Mountain in session. I did not imagine myself in a 'shivering society'. Writs, however, did not issue. The threat was sufficient to bring the Senate to its knees. Nor did I observe any notable 'sub-servience' when a little later I found myself at a function in the Aula Maxima at a period of schism in the Literary and Historical. Many of the students were still cross with their President. They gathered about Cruise O'Brien, protagonist in their quarrel, who had just come in, 'chaired' him with no great difficulty and proceeded in crocodile around the hall and then up the 'staircase, still singing 'God Save Ireland', to deposit him at length at the door of the President's Chamber. Here was no great care on anyone's part for expedient graces. This was, it is true, in 1905—three years after Joyce had left the College. The political atmosphere had sharpened; the university situation had grown more acute; but the temper of the students had not essentially changed. The young cocks were crowing as the old. The tune came from no 'shivering society' but from (I quote the most truthful and outspoken of the Irish Chief Secretaries, Augustine Birrell, who had a close-up experience of the College and saw the students in action) 'a very democratic assembly, by no means very docile and obviously not humble'.[1] I need develop this topic no further. Defence of my fellow-students is superfluous and distasteful, and if I have entered into it at all it is only by way of warning against the blind acceptance of *Stephen Hero* or the *Portrait of the Artist* as a transcript of college life, and to set up my own roadblock in the way of the odd mentality to which all Catholic education appears an obscurantist tyranny. Properly regarded, *Stephen Hero* has a high autobiographical as well as a literary interest. Not a vain coinage, though the author did his best to obliterate it and withhold it from currency.

It is appropriate to insert here the last of the Cornell letters—a letter written to Joyce in 1917 in acknowledgement of *A Portrait of the Artist*. Since the letter expresses, however summarily, my contemporary opinion, I shall not comment on it save in one respect: I have opened the way to a misconception by reproaching Joyce with unkindness in his references to our Dean of Studies. In using the words 'if harmless and pitiable' I am as certain as the lapse of time permits that I did not use this description as my own. It was never my opinion of the Dean. His idiosyncrasies certainly made him the butt of many stories, and much student mimicry, but we all not merely loved him for his invariable kindness but appreciated and respected his unique quality. It is inconceivable to me that I should ever have used these derogatives, which would explain themselves had I used inverted commas. I think Joyce understood them to be my echo or transcription of something he had himself said or written and that I had clumsily used to shorten argument.

> 15 Garville Avenue, Rathgar,
> Dublin. 26th Febr. 1917.

Dear Joyce,

I am immensely flattered to have from your publisher a copy of your novel and your note. The book is making itself felt and I am only afraid that a *succès de scandale* may obsure its proper virtue. I expect you will have seen by the time this letter reaches you Wells's review of it in the *Nation*. The notice, at the end at least, is amazingly stupid and unctuous but it praises the book highly and will unquestionably sell it. I do a little work at present for the *Nation* and on receiving the novel I wrote to interest Massingham in it and perhaps my letter helped the prompt review. Ezra Pound is doing another article on you for *The Egoist*.

[1] *Centenary History of the Literary and Historical Society, U.C.D.*, ed. Meenan, p. 317.

As to my own opinion of it—you have given it an excellent title and the only just criticism must have reference to it and so in regard to the desperate brutalities I am content with your 'this race, this country and this life produced me—I shall express myself as I am'. I admire, too, your courage in scrapping your first draft as I knew it. I think there were passages in that version which might well have been retained but as the chapters were being added to it, it seemed to me that the writer's mood was changing too much from the reminiscent Dichtung of the opening to the literalness and finally to the harshness of the latest chapters I saw. This version is all of a piece and is much more skilfully and economically worked out. But all the same I regret some episodes in *Stephen Hero*.

On the other hand I think that the student characters are too little individualized within their own group—a good deal of Cranly and Temple not excepted. To us who know them it is easy to distinguish them by personal tricks of speech but they all present too much the same kind of foil to the only character you were really interested in. Secondly I think the pages on aesthetics are too dead, mainly because you talk them at Lynch. I rather think it is a pity that for that side you didn't make Stephen use the old Debating Society. Then I think you are unjust in almost alone mentioning Ghezzi by name and you are unkind to the dean of studies who after all was a kind if harmless and pitiable soul.

But I can't sufficiently praise the fine things. It was a continual pleasure to see so much of the old days in literature—the old songs, 'Turpin Hero', 'Pastime with Good Company'—not so very good perhaps—and the ancient scornfulness. But there were passages of unalloyed joy in the exquisite feeling for words—the girl at the North Bull p. 199 and all that episode; the dance at pp. 257-258, her hand 'a soft merchandise' and the gorgeous thrifty adverb at the top of p. 271. Surely we can still hope for another volume of Chamber Music or rather not Chamber Music but fine poetry none the less when you are still writing these pages or such others as the birds in Kildare St. (Kildare St. by the way reminds me that you have made a mistake in planting the Royal Irish Academy in the passage from 'the duke's lawn' to the National Library. You meant the School of Art.)

I hope to hear from you sometime that you are still writing verse, I have one poem of yours in MS., and to hear of another book. The fact that you have left the whole Abbey Theatre group out in the cold—at which they will scarcely repine—suggests that another volume of unamiable observation is threatening. I cannot help thinking from much of the *Portrait* and from *Chamber Music* that when that book is done with you will put that class of work definitely behind you and quarry something less dependent on externals out of your own imagination and deeper experience. I would be glad to hear from you on what you are doing. I have heard vague reports that your eyes have been giving you very serious trouble, and better news to the effect that American publishers are looking for your work. I hope the second is truer than the first.

With best wishes.   Sincerely yours,   C. P. Curran

There has been since a favourable one column review in the *Manchester Guardian* of Friday March 2nd and another in the *Times Literary Supplement* of the same week.

Jimmy Good was on the staff of the *Freeman's Journal* at this date, with John Hooper as the editor. He told (an unconfirmed) story of how John Stanislaus Joyce came to the office one evening with a copy of the *Portrait of the Artist* which had just been published, saw the editor, and asked for the favour of an early review of 'his son's first novel'. When John Stanislaus left the editor sent for Jimmy Good who did not happen to be in the office. A subordinate appeared and when the editor was assured that the type had not been 'locked up' he told him to write a review for the next day's issue. The reviewer was going out for his supper. Over sandwiches and beer with his friends he quite forgot the urgency of his commission. Remembering, he rushed back to the office, hurriedly opened the book at the sermon on hell, read, turned over a few more following pages of an edifying character and began his review, 'This is a book which should be in every Catholic home . . .', and so forth. Jimmy Good said that hardened *Freeman's Journal* men blushed to hear the story.

After Joyce and I had taken our Modern Literature degrees in the autumn of 1902, Joyce, as I have mentioned, went to Paris and stayed near the Luxembourg at the Hotel Corneille. It was a modest hotel, celebrated by Thackeray and Du Maurier, but it had earlier and later associations that were purely Irish. Father Prout had lived there, and John Mitchel and John O'Leary and in my own time Synge and Stephen MacKenna; Joyce, no doubt, went to it by reason of its Dublin connections. I stayed there myself later, on the recommendation of some friend of Dr. Sigerson's circle, probably Stephen MacKenna whose way of living there was not less Spartan than Joyce's—he lived, he said, on what he borrowed from Synge, while Synge lived on what he got back from MacKenna, I heard nothing of Joyce from Paris, and, occupied with my own affairs and new studies, saw nothing of him until his mother's death in 1903, and I did not follow all his reviews—some sixteen in number

—which were printed in the Dublin *Daily Express* from December 1902 to the following November. Another one—of Ibsen's *Catilina*—was printed in *The Speaker* (London).

These reviews deserve attention. They are composed with uniform care and deliberation. Written at a low ebb in his fortune, they show no trace of haste or half-work. They have complete assurance with due sense of responsibility, occasionally harsh but more usually written with courtesy or a politeness touched with irony. Naturally they reveal the course of his reading and his earlier studies. One of the slighter notices begins with Da Vinci's observation on the tendency of the mind to impose its own likeness upon that which it creates. All show this trait, whether in his indiscriminate eulogy of Bruno, in his unfavourable comparison of Goldsmith's arcadian grace with Crabbe's realism, in his scornful attack on Schiller's pragmatism, or in his sympathy with the wise, passive philosophy of the Burmese and their table of values: happiness founded on peace of mind in all circumstances, the courtesies of life not neglected, all anger and rudeness kept at a distance. And apt epithets are not missing, as when he writes of the agent of the papish plot as 'the monstrous, moon-faced leader—the horrible Oates'.

The articles on Bruno and on Lady Gregory's *Poets and Dreamers* as well as the short, trenchant notice of William Rooney's poems go back to Joyce's Mangan paper, just as the *Catilina* review with its discounting of the Romantic temper and the breaking-up of tradition draws possibly from 'Drama and Life'. All clearly indicate his detachment from national propaganda and our folklore literature. He repudiates both Rooney's patriotic verse and the stories of 'feeble and sleepy' minds brought back by Lady Gregory from her exploration of a 'land almost fabulous in its sorrow and senility'. Yet in this censure of her twilight art he was neither a precursor nor did he stand alone. He was speaking his own convictions confirmed by Ibsen, but he was also repeating what Kettle had said five years earlier when, deriding the literary wardrobe of this art, he found it 'groping in the dust and shrouds of the past not for the lost thread of the labyrinth [of true progress] but for the sorry tinsel of folklore and legend to dress them up for the stranger—a retrospective renaissance with no manly vigour, no spring of action, no fruit but Dead Sea fruit'. The stringency of Joyce's criticism was not lessened by his not being alone in this particular judgement and hardly softened further either by his scorn for Whistler's nocturnes and Mallarmé's verse or, on the other hand, by his studied reservation in favour of Yeats's 'delicate scepticism'. At any rate, this review article (which, unlike the others, was signed or at least initialled) defined clearly enough his relation with our new school of writers and his distance from the majority of his brother bards.

This was also his brief period of dissipation, a dissipation quite foreign to his character. His fortunes were at their lowest ebb. The breakwater of order was less evident than the squalor against which he had sought to build it and to many outsiders it was not plain that there was in fact any citadel to defend. He had published little or nothing: they saw only a 'troop of unmannerly passions'—defiant flags on sand-hills; pretensions and little substance; much cry and no wool. Even the herdsmen of slow, twilight flocks grew impatient and some, angry. Ever since, the amateurs at a distance from the *vie de Bohème* have been fascinated by the violent contrast presented by the heaven-aspiring artist's excursions into taverns and brothels. Their picture of a twentieth-century Dublin Villon or Verlaine is grossly exaggerated. In the first place, the interval of loose living was quite short: it can be reckoned barely in months. It may also be measured quite prosaically in terms of cash and hard work. From the autumn when his home was broken up Joyce was living from hand to mouth, his meals scanty and precarious. A few hours a week of teaching, a handful of reviews, two short stories, three poems, an odd concert engagement, paid or unpaid at Dublin current rates, afforded little margin for excess once landladies' bills were paid. This work of his was punctually discharged and with scrupulous care, while he was still finding time for some musical training. And to this must be added the steadily accumulating mass of the *Stephen Hero* MS. The account does not square with much hectic living, but what there was of it was sufficiently startling, being lived openly and in defiance of convention, and was in plain contradication with his life before and after the winter and spring of 1903-4. Reckless as he seemed, Joyce never threw down the reins of will. His whole nature was bent excessively in the contrary direction, being perpetually and often preposterously given to method and to elaborate planning, much of it miraculously executed.

It was at this time, in the summer of 1904, that I took the photograph, mentioned above, in the garden of my father's home and in reference to which Edmund Wilson in *Axel's Castle* queried whether without it we should ever have a clear idea of Stephen Dedalus. He also appears in a group of my fellow-students and professors in two other photographs I took in 1902. Both these groups were taken on the same occasion. Having exposed the first plate, I took my position in the second and got the college porter to squeeze the bulb. The photos were taken in the grounds behind the College (Nos. 85 and 86 Stephen's Green) and beside the ball alley mentioned in the *Portrait of the Artist*. The 1904 photograph has a certain humorous bravado in dress and carriage and the same quality, with something more affecting, appears in four notes to me which have survived the vicissitudes of many years. Two I have already quoted in connexion with the *Stephen Hero* MS. The third is a postcard with the postmark of 3 July 1904. It runs:

Je serai à votre bureau demain. Suis dans un trou sanguinaire.

J. A. J.

And the fourth:

60 Shelbourne Road.
30th August 1904.

My dear Curran,
 I am in double trouble, mental and material. Can you meet me to-morrow at half past four at smoke-room Bewley's in Westmoreland Street?

Yours truly,
J. A. Joyce

This letter of 30 August 1904 is the last I had from him before he left Dublin with his future wife for Pola and Trieste. I do not recollect the precise circumstances which provoked it, but I do remember my own bewilderment when Joyce characteristically reminded me thirty years afterwards of what passed between us at that meeting— giving its exact date and place. Nor did I know anything of his fortunate engagement to Nora Barnacle until he came to me one day in October to tell me of their resolution to leave Dublin.

 As I have mentioned, I had seen comparatively little of Joyce in 1903 or in the first months of 1904. I had been to Italy for some four or five weeks in February and March and he left Cabra to occupy the Martello Tower at Sandycove with Oliver Gogarty and Chenevix Trench. I did not see him at the Tower nor, indeed until he had moved to Shelbourne Road and was beginning his singing lessons. Nor except for casual meetings, did I really know Trench for another year, though I was to see a good deal of him when with John Marcus O'Sullivan we had entered the Kings' Inns and were attending our first year's law lectures in Trinity College. I can in no way recognize him in the Haines of *Ulysses* and he should not be so identified with him. Trench was an Irishman who had come over from Oxford and grew interested in the Theatre and language movement. He was on the committee of the Theatre of Ireland and as an amateur played the part of O'Hanrahan in Douglas Hyde's *Casadh an t-Súgáin*. As law students at T.C.D., the three of us listened to scholarly lectures on obsolete feudal law from the ageing but hardy pedestrian Vaughan Hart and with growing indifference we disregarded young Robert Leonard as he sleeked his glossy hair and droned out criminal law. We were more interested in the theatre. We pooled our play-books: John Marcus O'Sullivan fresh from Germany, contributed much Hauptmann, Sudermann, and Ibsen; Trench contributed Shaw and Pinero; and I myself, Maeterlinck and the French dramatists, with more Ibsen. In one term we consumed the European stage, taking a few hours off at the end to run through Stephen's *Digest* before a perfunctory examination. But of the future author of *Ulysses* I heard nothing from Trench.

It was plain enough to me in that autumn that Joyce was at a dead end and that even with the prop of some auxiliary post he could not live in Dublin as the writer he meant to be. In Joyce's family circumstances—with a father who even in middle years had thrown over his responsibility for a numerous family and built all his hopes for himself and them on his eldest son—the situation was quite impossible. Even if the father was not quite the human boa-constrictor of the Mangan paper, even if he was less extraordinary than he was, Joyce was unfitted for that burden. His father has since become something of a legendary character, but the legend hardly outruns the facts. I knew him only in his last days, though like many north-side Dubliners I was familiar with his bristly, stocky figure in the Prince Albert and low topper worn by men of his generation (though in his case the top hat and frock-coat, spruce enough on the first of the month, grew a bit seedy towards its close). He had passed in his time from one employment to another before renouncing all, but his mainstay was a pension of some £250 a year drawn for Government service in the abolished office of the Collector-General of Taxes. Apropos his rate collection, a friend of his told me one story which appears to date from the time the Joyces were living close to Eccles Street at 29 Hardwicke Street. 'Jack', as he was known to his friends, had to get in the Eccles Street rates and he decided he would save himself a lot of trouble by serving court summonses straight away for non-payment of rates, before the regular notices to pay were issued. Court-day came, and Jack attended the Magistrates Court to get his decrees or his money. Then for the first time he discovered, to his horror, that on his list of alleged defaulters was the magistrate himself who, he knew, was in no affluent circumstances. Before the cases were called the magistrate had a hurried word with him, said he noticed his own name on the list, that this was awkward and indecorous, but that he could assure him that his rates in default would be promptly forthcoming. Greatly relieved, Mr. Joyce said: 'Of course, of course, any time at your convenience, etc.' Then the application came on for hearing and one householder, appearing indignantly, produced his receipt for payment. To the enormous relief of Mr. Joyce the magistrate rapidly intervened, 'We all know that Mr. Joyce is a most capable and conscientious officer. Decree granted.' If his character had been different, John Stanislaus would have been a remarkable social figure in Dublin life. As it was, even during Joyce's school-days his way of living drove him down to always lower levels, commuting fraction after fraction of his pension and insurance policy until little was left to supplement the rent of the house he had once bought in St. Peters Road, Cabra. He passed from lodging to lodging, paying no bills, and dragging after him in his flight his hapless family. This was the position when Joyce was at college. One story I had of a time when they were at Fairview lodging with a Frenchman named Bosinnet. The father and he collaborated in non-payment of rent but when forced to leave a house after some months Bosinnet, posing as landlord, would recommend Joyce senior as a most desirable, punctually paying tenant and John Stanislaus would enter into possession of the new premises with Bosinnet as his lodger and so on alternately. Another tale told of a night's drinking with friends when he had been living far out beyond Clontarf. Helpless and protesting, he was pushed into the last Dolly-mount tram and put in charge of the conductor. Faithful to his trust and in spite of all protests, the conductor allowed him to alight only when at midnight they had reached Dollymount. His friends met him the next day and made due inquiries as to how he got home. His language was more than usually fearful; unknown to them, a day or two earlier and in customary haste, he had moved camp to Phibsboro, a quite other quarter of the city.

He was a man of unparalleled vituperative power, a virtuoso in speech with unique control of the vernacular, his language often coarse and blasphemous to a degree of which, in the long run, he could hardly himself have been conscious. A notable singer, with a wide knowledge of Italian opera, he would hold the attention of any room all night if there was a piano at which he could sit, play, and sing. He could fascinate indefinitely with stories told with consummate art, one neatly fitting into another. And these stories would be of a perfectly drawing-room character till suddenly, as if taken unawares, he would slip into the coarse vein and another side of his nature and vocabulary be revealed.

He was living in this shiftless way long prior to his wife's death in 1903, his family the victim of that tempestuous nature portrayed so admirably by Patrick Tuohy in his portrait of the septuagenarian, where after the lenitive of seventy years the volcano still more than smoulders. He was imposing a quite intolerable strain on those family ties and obligations which in Ireland perhaps more than elsewhere are freely recognized. It was not at all that mutual affection was lacking in the Joyce household or—at least from one side—an exact understanding. At home or on long walks with the two elder boys he had been an inexhaustible reservoir of song and story and racy commentary on life. To his latest days Joyce, like his sisters, spoke of the old man with the same despairing, humorous affection and appreciation, and his more poignant feeling overflows in his 'Ecce Puer' and the closing pages of *Finnegans Wake*. But he could do little to alleviate the misery which followed his mother's death, when his father was a broken man. Deprived of her gentle restraint, demoralization set in and his family, powerless to help, gradually scattered. Presently there was complete collapse, and the old man suffered ignominy before he was at length rescued by friends like Alf Bergan and the Medcalfes, generous, understanding, and forbearing good Samaritans, who took him into their care for his last twelve years or more. All this lay in the future. He was now in the bankrupt stage of his career, accurately enough detailed by Stephen towards the close of the *Portrait of the Artist*. For Joyce in 1904 there was no outlet but flight; whatever assistance he might give his family could be rendered from a distance, and it was fortunate for him and for us that it was in the June of this year that he met the woman whose courage and devotion confirmed his resolution to leave Dublin and saw him safely through the difficult years that lay before him. They left Dublin together on 8 October on their way to

Pola, where he had been offered a post in a Berlitz school for languages.

It so happened that my friend James Murnaghan and I had already arranged to spend the first fortnight of that month in Paris. Economically we travelled by night and by the Dieppe boat, where there was much talk of Pretty Polly's chances in the *Grand Prix* to be run the next day at Longchamps, and our first conversation at 6 a.m. with the *garçon de chambre* at the Pension Orfilas in the Rue d'Assas was on that momentous topic. Next morning Joyce called to see me as he had promised, but of that meeting I have little other memory than the sudden view of his familiar profile passing the window where we sat after breakfast. We had a later meeting at a café and parted in the Rue Monsieur le Prince where he was staying, but I did not then meet Nora and our talk was only of his prospects by the Adriatic.

That was the last I saw of him for five or six years. We kept up a desultory correspondence sometimes upon the appearance of articles of his in the Trieste *Piccolo della Sera*. One of these which he sent me, 'L'Ultimo Feniano', was occasioned by the death in 1907 of John O'Leary. In the same year I had from him *Chamber Music* with the following letter:

Via S. Nicolo. 32. IIIo
Trieste (Austria)

Dear Curran,

I send you by the same post my volume of verses *Chamber Music* which was published in London on Monday last. I trust sincerely that in the future I may be in a position to requite the obligations I am under towards you. I would have sent you also my MS copy but that I feared my doing so would seem to imply a higher conceit of these verses than I now have. However if you wish for it (as I promised it to you) I have it still.

Faithfully Yours

10 May 1907   Jas. A. Joyce

Re-reading this letter, I am desolated not to have promptly seized upon his generous offer of the MS. of these verses. The explanation probably lies in a note to me some weeks later from Stanislaus telling me that his brother had been laid up for more than a month with rheumatic fever and eye trouble. His first brief visit to Ireland in 1909 was in the long vacation when I was not in town, and although he was back again for some months in the following winter as an advance agent to set up the Volta Cinema in Mary

Street—the first of a numerous Dublin brood—and I met him not infrequently, my only recollection is of his singing from the score of *Manon Lescaut* and of talk of Massenet and Puccini. His final visit was in 1912, when I was called off the sidelines to take a very casual part in the *Dubliners* imbroglio. Joyce had been to his solicitor about his contract with Maunsel & Co. and George Roberts, and he was of the opinion that the solicitor might be fortified by my opinion of the texts in dispute. Three of the stories had already appeared in the *Irish Homestead* and he now gave me the entire page proofs to read, without comment or any indication as to where the trouble was brewing. During our interview with the solicitor Joyce remained remarkably silent and the solicitor was obviously ill at ease upon unfamiliar ground. We went over the text, the hard-boiled, police-court solicitor showing sensitive reaction to much of its vulgar language. Though I myself was a bit dubious only on the score of 'An Encounter', my view was that no prosecution was anywhere likely and that the public authorities would remain supremely indifferent to its publication. I was surprised and a little amused to find that, amongst all the episodes in question, 'An Encounter' seemed to have aroused the least misgiving. A relic of this interview survives in Joyce's letter to me of August 1912 written immediately before his final departure

19th August 1912   17 Richmond Place N/C/R.
                                                                    Dublin.

Dear Curran

Allow me to thank you before you leave Dublin for your very kind intervention to-day on my behalf and also to wish you a pleasant holiday abroad. Should you be near the 'amaro Adriatico' I hope you will come also to my poor Trieste.

With kind regards and remembrances.

Sincerely yours
James Joyce

3

Joyce Leaves Dublin

JOYCE left Dublin in 1904 not as an Aristides driven out by his fellow-citizens but 'self doomed and unafraid'. He was primarily a victim of economics, his departure the inevitable outcome of his circumstances—in the heel of the reel Shem the Penman out of a job would sit and write. To write he had to escape from the situation created by his father, and to help him do so there came to his side at the critical moment the woman he made his wife. Shem the Penman's problem could only be solved outside Ireland and if he had simply gone to London like many of his contemporaries to pick up work as a journalist and conventional man of letters, his departure would everywhere have been regarded as quite normal. It would have excited no comment, then or later. English critics would have seen it to be in the natural order of things. We should have heard nothing of exile from them, and American expatriates would not have identified it with their own flight from Gopher Prairies. The Greenwich meridian, however, did not run through University College. Italy or France, if not Scandinavia, was Joyce's natural *locus refugii*; the timely offer of a teaching post brought him to Italian-speaking Pola. As always, he went where he could live and write with least disturbance. When he was living in Paris years later, in the full tide of work, he could still write to his friend Frank Budgen, 'Can you tell a poor hard-working man where is the ideal climate inhabited by ideal humans.' He never knew that land, though the go-as-you-please of Paris made it his longest and most congenial abode. I do not pretend that his was not a spiritual as well as an economic exile. He was everywhere an exile of the soul, and an inner detachment made his departure from Dublin all the easier. When I met him in Paris on his way to Pola with Nora, there was certainly no resentful casting of his shoe over Edom. He was as Gabriel in his own story, 'The Dead': 'He felt they had escaped from their lives and duties, escaped from home and friends and run away together with wild and radiant hearts to a new adventure.' Like Falk in Ibsen's play: 'Out into God's world he carried within his breast a two-stringed lute. The upper string vibrated to the joy of life, the lower had its own secret notes quivering long and deep.'[1]

I do not ignore the parting shafts of his 'Holy Office' let loose against some of his acquaintance. My note to him in August 1904 (quoted on pp. 46–47) gives ample reason to think the lines were written independently of his departure. At any rate they were earlier in their sharpening and unlike the 'Millennial Ode' which Ibsen wrote in flight. The squib which had been offered me for *St. Stephen's* is no more than a tart *jeu d'esprit*. It is obviously of a quite different origin from the 'Gas from a Burner', written twelve years later, which singed Maunsel and Falconer with a more scorching flame. That burner was first lit by an English publisher and English printers. His misadventures with them inflamed his later trouble at home with Maunsel and his printer, and this quarrel in the long run became for him a symbol, magnifying the trolls which always beleaguered his imagination. The trolls he divined in Dublin he was to find ubiquitous. As he presented them—and as they were more and more inflated by some contemporaries—Ireland appears as their unique habitat and their victim an Ishmael driven into exile.

Much of the writing of these commentators is negligible, arising from ignorance or preconceptions. What Stanislaus Joyce has written comes, however, with a different authority—by reason of his early intimacy and his own literary capacity. His critical discernment however, and the admiration in which he held his brother's early work do not exclude a great deal of prejudice, some bitterness, and much misconception of the Ireland to which from 1905 until his death he was an utter stranger. His elder brother watched Irish affairs from abroad with interest. He maintained many contacts with his homeland; Stanislaus had none outside his family, and in his later years he had comparatively little communication with his elder brother. At all times he gave heated expression to his opinions on Irish contemporaries and these *boutades*, whether his own or shared between them, I take with some reserve. They were the habitual rhetorical exercises in the vernacular 'contraps', in Joyce's phrase, 'of fermented words'.

[1] *Love's Comedy*, Act III.

In part I see them as an inheritance with which, on the shores of the *amaro Adriatico*, they comforted themselves in the racy accents of their father.

In his *Recollections*[1] Stanislaus Joyce describes the relations he supposes to have existed in 1904 between his brother and those whom he calls 'the other writers of what later became the Celtic revival'. His statements are definite and categorical. He finds amongst Joyce's fellow writers a latent hostility arising first because he separated himself from any purely national movement and later from their consciousness of his superiority to them in culture, talent, and moral courage; and again he writes: 'At a time when he had all the little literary world of Dublin against him, when his every activity was balked and everything that came from his pen was censored. . . .'

In these years from 1902 I was familiar with the figure of Stanislaus Joyce, long-coated, buttoned up, and with collar upturned, accompanying his brother on evening perambulations through the city. He had not been a student at college. He seemed to me a silent, devoted companion, imitating his brother's manner but standing apart when Joyce met an acquaintance. I never saw him except when alone or with his brother. On the few occasions I had speech with him, it was as his brother's emissary and, so far as my observation went, he had no acquaintance with Joyce's literary friends. His judgement of them, I must think, was formed at a distance out of youthful loyalty and later coloured not only by his own strong prejudices, but, more reasonably, by Oliver Gogarty's writings after Joyce's death. I do not know how far Gogarty's hostility was latent before the emergence of Buck Mulligan in *Ulysses*—I do not think there was any. But, with that single reservation, I find no truth at all in Stanislaus's sweeping charges and I speak from personal acquaintance with, I believe, every one of the writers concerned. If, furthermore, I were to seek out Gogarty's opinion of Joyce at this date, I would resurrect one of the many limericks in which he poked fun at his friends. It was written about 1903:

> There is a weird spectre called Joyce
> Re-arisen from Monasterboice
> His whole occupation

[1] Most of what I have written in this chapter was written before the appearance of Stanislaus Joyce's *My Brother's Keeper*. I have the less hesitation in disputing his statements since some of them were the subject of friendly interchange between us in his last years.

A walking negation
Of all his acquaintance's choice.

Not a very hostile manifestation one would say; in no way different
from limericks he wrote at the same time on his other friends, e.g.
Tom Kettle and A.E.,[1] or from Shem the Penman's description of
himself as one of those who 'sleep at our vigil and fast for our feast'
(*Finnegans Wake*, p. 189) or from the confession with which
Stanislaus concludes his own paper: 'I admit without hesitation that
Joyce was a very difficult person.'

I take a more explicit illustration to show the light in which his
own generation saw Joyce at this period. It is from the review of
Joyce's *Chamber Music* in the *Freeman's Journal* written on Saturday
1 June 1907 by Tom Kettle, the clearest voice in our college group
and representative of his literary generation:

Those who remember University College life of five years back will have
many memories of Mr. Joyce. Wilful, fastidious, a lover of elfish paradoxes
he was to the men of his time the very voice and embodiment of the
literary spirit. His work, never very voluminous had from the first a rare
and exquisite accent. One still goes back to the files of *St. Stephen's*, the
Saturday Review, the [*Irish*] *Homestead* and to various occasional maga-
zines to find those lyrics and stories which, though at first reading, so
slight and frail still held one by their integrity of form. *Chamber Music* is
a collection of the best of these delicate verses which have, each of them,

---

[1] On Tom Kettle:

A holy Hegelian Kettle
Has faith which we cannot unsettle
If no one abused it
He might have reduced it
But now he is quite on his mettle.

On A.E.:

There is a weird poet called Russell
Who wouldn't eat even a mussel
When chased by an oyster
He ran to a cloister
Away from the beef and the bustle.

The cloister he called the 'Hermetic'
I found it a fine diuretic
A most energetic
And mental emetic
Heretic, prophetic, ascetic.

the bright beauty of a crystal. The title of the book evokes the atmosphere of remoteness, restraint, accomplished execution characteristic of the whole contents. There is but one theme behind the music, a love gracious and in its way strangely intense but fashioned by temperamental and literary moulds too strict to permit it to pass ever into the great tumult of passion. The inspiration of the book is almost entirely literate. There is no trace of the folklore, the folk-dialect or even the national feeling that have coloured the work of practically every writer in contemporary Ireland. Neither is there any sense of that modern point of view which consumes all life in the language of 'problems'. It is clear, delicate, distinguished playing of the same kindred with wood birds and with Paul Verlaine. But the only possible criticism of poetry is quotation.

Briefly reviewing Irish literature for 1907, the Sinn Fein *Irish Year Book* mentions *Chamber Music* as proof of Joyce's 'very delightful and delicate lyric talent'. I ingeminate that here again there is no evidence of hostility, latent or overt, in my parish or of ostracism, any more than in the matter of 'The Day of the Rabblement' and its *amende honorable* in the publication of 'Mangan', with which I have dealt earlier. If this was the attitude of Joyce's immediate contemporaries between 1901 and 1907, how did his seniors react to the publication in 1901 of this first raking attack on their literary programme? How far did they attempt to balk his activity? Having no evidence, I pass over the mention in *Stephen Hero* of an offer by the University College authorities of some tutorial work about 1902. I never heard of it, but Mr. Mason apparently refers to it as a Jesuit lure.[1] Quite as jesuitically, and at the same date, Yeats introduced Joyce to Arthur Symons and used all his good offices to open for him the doors of London editors. George Moore's dramatic work was the target of Joyce's sharper criticism, but neither then nor at any later time did Moore show any resentment. Quite the contrary, and when it fell to him to express a literary judgement there was no trace of hostility. He came to his support later in the matter of a Civil List pension when Joyce's fortunes were at a very low ebb. Writing with some reserve on his other stories, he said that 'The Dead' seemed to him perfection when he read it and regretted he was not its author. Joyce in his turn, suffering no wrong, but inheriting, rather, Moore's 'mimetic ability', harboured no ill feeling. He did not, in fact, meet Moore until a few years before his elder's

[1] Stanislaus Joyce and Ellsworth Mason, *The Early Joyce: Book Reviews 1902-3* (Colorado Springs, 1955), p. 30.

death. Writing on that occasion, he expressed the hope that he paid him 'the respect due to his age, personality and achievement'. To Yeats, as is well-known, he showed on all occasions a special courtesy and regard. He never failed to acknowledge the debt he was under to him.

A.E. has received unmannerly and undeserved treatment at Stanislaus Joyce's hands on the same score. But, in this critical year (1904) of his departure from Dublin, A.E. printed three stories by Joyce in the *Irish Homestead* which later appeared in *Dubliners* and subsequently one of his poems. The *Daily Express* had been printing his reviews for twelve months before and *Dana*, edited by John Eglinton and Fred Ryan, had published one of his poems. It is true that *Dana* declined the offer in 1904 of some draft or introductory chapter of *Stephen Hero*. John Eglinton has left his account, which I have given above in Chapter 2, of the proffer of this bulky MS. In declining it he did not overstep an ordinary editorial function nor did it appear so to Joyce then or later, when his comment to Miss Harriet Weaver on *Stephen Hero* was succinct but humorously unjust to himself: 'What rubbish it is.'

What becomes, then, of his brother's wild statement that everything that came from Joyce's pen at this date—about 1904—was censored and that he had all the little literary world of Dublin against him?

His other charges of concerted Catholic or nationalist intolerance are more profuse, equally unfounded, contradictory, and wholly ill-defined. A.E. was a nationalist and a theosophist. T. P. Gill was a nationalist and a Catholic and though he had just relinquished his editorship of the *Daily Express* it was he who had made it one of the champions of the new theatre movement and had settled its literary attitude. John Eglinton and Fred Ryan, in their conduct of *Dana*, were declared anti-clericals, but John Eglinton was an imperialist and Fred Ryan a socialist and nationalist of the same temper as Frank Skeffington and in his outlook not very far removed from Joyce himself. In this variety of opinion, where is the evidence or likelihood, amongst either Joyce's seniors or his equals, of a banded hostility?

Stanislaus Joyce's charge reaches egregious expression when, after the long-drawn-out discussion and ultimate breakdown of the contract with Grant Richards, *Dubliners* was offered to the Irish firm of Maunsel. Into the ensuing Maunsel–Falconer tangle he introduces an imaginary 'vigilance committee . . . presided over by the Viceroy's wife, but the Jesuits were widely represented on it, both directly and indirectly',[1] at whose behest the edition was destroyed.[2] I can only stare and gasp at this nonsense. This indeed is 'bodiless ecstasy' *à la* Eugène Sue or such as possessed the begetter of the rule in *MacNaghten's Case* wherein an Ulsterman, conceiving himself the victim of a conspiracy between Peel, the Pope, and the Jesuits, assassinated Peel's secretary in mistake for the Prime Minister.

I have nothing to say in defence of the ambiguous transactions which culminated in the precipitate destruction by the printer of the sheets of *Dubliners*. It was a harsh experience for Joyce in the house of his friends and left its permanent mark. However rough the deal, there is no reason to import into it any political or sectarian bias. The directors of the publishing firm and their printer were, as it happened, of three or four different religions and of equally varied brands of politics and their behaviour did not differ materially from Grant Richards's hesitations, prolonged over nine years from 1905, and the recalcitrance of the English printers. There is nothing in the history of publishing that makes the Maunsel story exceptional. Watchdog biting dog, Thackeray closed down Ruskin in the *Cornhill* and Froude stopped him in *Frasers*. Leslie Stephen censored Hardy in the *Cornhill*, Mudie banned Meredith, and Dreiser was withdrawn after publication. Max Beerbohm did not escape scratching and the B.B.C. and the Home Office were later to make difficulties for Joyce. Those things being so, I see no reason why my parish should be the peculiar butt of obloquy or why Stanislaus Joyce should reiterate direful assertions of hidden forces and hands raised in darkness against his brother. The simple explanation of caution on the part of printer and publisher, dubious of their legal position, was not, at any rate, accepted by him.

Joyce's own resentment helped to colour his record of earlier happenings when, in the company of Stanislaus, he was reducing the MS. of *Stephen Hero* into *A Portrait of the Artist as a Young Man*. Both of them saw all Irish affairs in the light of an inherited family trait which cannot fairly be ignored. A corrosive, sceptical suspicion was a characteristic of the father. It appears in Joyce's delineation of him. Stanislaus, recognizing it in himself, wrote, 'My character is permeated with suspicion.'[3] This element of suspicion cropped up in Joyce's own talk with disconcerting frequency though usually with

---

[1] *Recollections*, p. 9.
[2] *The Listener*, 25 March 1954.
[3] Stanislaus Joyce, *Dublin Diary* (London, 1962), ed. Healy, p. 38.

a comic twist. Joyce recognized it in himself in *Stephen Hero* as 'the divining of intrigue' and as part of the 'ineradicable egoism' that conceived all the thoughts and deeds of his microcosm as converging on himself. The sensitive victim beheld 'the pack of enmities come tumbling and sniffing . . . after their game', and as Shem the Penman the tragic jester mocked in himself the dislocated reasoner, the seeker of the nest of evil in a good word, the blind porer over suspicion and auguries (*Finnegans Wake*, p. 189). This faculty of divination lay dangerously close to persecution mania. I say this with difficulty, conscious as I am of the genuine obstacle against which he resolutely struggled and of his own share in creating them. It had early, preposterous expression in his appeal to Lady Gregory in 1902.[1] The same charge of 'a deliberate conspiracy of certain forces in Ireland to silence me' is repeated to the London publisher, Elkin Mathews, in 1913[2] but it gains no greater force by his complaint in 1921 that he has then 'been a year in Paris and in that time not a word about me has appeared in any French periodical'.[3] It was a trait which was only gradually coming to my notice and was in later years to make me often stare at him in bewilderment. Living abroad, it was fed by ill-formed, perhaps obsequious, gossip. Paradoxically, the sceptic was too often credulous. Joyce in Paris was like Ibsen in Dresden, of whom it is written that 'he missed not one item of anything written or said or whispered about him in Norway or elsewhere even though it were spoken in Chocktaw at some Burmese altar'.[4] He attached importance to scribblers and their wildest inventions made a permanent lodgement. He had little sense of proportion either in what concerned his own work or in his activities on behalf of his friends. When his interest in the theatre brought him into relation with the English Players in Zürich and into a complicated row with a British Consul, he sent to me, as to others in 1919, a long dossier on the affair for urgent publication. At that time I was Irish Correspondent for the *Nation* and I mentioned the matter to its editor, H. W. Massingham, as well as to Jimmy Good, the Irish Correspondent of the *New Statesman*, and to the *Freeman's Journal*. Nothing, so far as I recollect, followed at either end. Joyce took this silence as deliberate indifference. He made small account of

[1] Stuart Gilbert (ed.), *Letters of James Joyce* (London, 1957), p. 53.
[2] ibid., p. 73.
[3] ibid., p. 166.
[4] Edmund Gosse, *Life of Ibsen* (London, 1908).

the absorption of Ireland in its own acute revolutionary business and could still think it possible his little rumpus in a Zürich office had an interest for a Dublin editor who was about to see his printing-press smashed up by the Black and Tans. When his wife and family were travelling in a Galway train carrying soldiers during our subsequent civil commotions, this train was fired on and his family flung themselves on the floor of their compartment. Joyce persuaded himself that the attack had an ulterior motive and, incredible as it sounds, that he was being aimed at through his family. I do not yet know whether I succeeded in disabusing his mind. Equally, he is reported as believing some silly, quite groundless, story that his books were burned at some date or another on the steps of the National University, by which I suppose was meant University College, Dublin. One could multiply such instances of credulity. Some were entertained in pure ignorance; some were wrong deductions from a grain of fact; many were mere dialectical perversions thrown at one's head by way of humorous retort. But, whether well- or ill-founded, they did live in corners of his mind as symbols of forces gathered in the shadows against him, and, if it were not for his own stronger will and his antiseptic humour and for his wife's gay and unfailing commonsense, they might have taken a more tragic turn.

I recall Rousseau in Byron's words of *Childe Harold*:

> His life was one long war with self-sought foes,
> Or friends by him self-banish'd; for his mind
> Had grown Suspicion's sanctuary, and chose,
> For its own cruel sacrifice, the kind,
> 'Gainst whom he raged with fury strange and blind.
> But he was phrensied,—wherefore, who may know?
> Since cause might be which skill could never find;
> But he was phrensied by disease or woe,
> To that worst pitch of all, which wears a reasoning show.:[1]

Such misconceptions give rise to others, as the Surinam toad sprouts as it goes. It is regrettable, however, that they still find credit in the minds of competent critics. Writing to me in 1940 on the publication of *Finnegans Wake*, Joyce found its most curious notice to come from a Finn in Helsinki and the best from Professor Levin of Harvard. Professor Levin's later book confirms Joyce's tribute and I read, therefore, with all the more astonishment its statement that

[1] *Childe Harold*, III, 80.

'Joyce's books could not and cannot be published or sold in his native country'.[1] I have dealt with his early pamphlet 'The Day of Rabblement', published in Dublin in 1901. As to all his other writing, it is incorrect to say that any book that Joyce ever issued could not at any time or cannot be bought and sold in market overt in the Republic of Ireland. For a few months, but a few months only, *Stephen Hero* was on the index of books prohibited by the Censorship Board. No other book of Joyce's was ever banned by the Board, though it is true that the customs authorities—acting under a British Parliament Act of 1878 stopped *Ulysses* at the port of entry on several occasions.

During Joyce's two visits to Dublin after 1904 I saw no trace of any resentment towards his old associates apart from the quarrel with Maunsel & Co. Absent from Dublin in the long vacation of 1909, as I have mentioned, I saw comparatively little of him at that time. The Volta Cinema project was then occupying his main attention and his friends were naturally intrigued at his sudden appearance in this new role as a man of business, which he took very seriously. Whenever we met, there seemed little in him of the dedicated man of letters, and the evenings went in music and talk of opera. In 1912 he was still the man of business concentrated exclusively on discussion of the Maunsel affair. His resentment, however, went no further than the four corners of his contract. I heard nothing of the language of the embittered exile but very much indeed of the iniquities of publishers. The change from his student years was apparent. The reserve which was second nature to him had become more marked. His self-possession had grown even greater, but there was nothing at all of the artificial aloofness of the early D'Annunzian *sovrouomo*. In company there was little talk of literature and, though his talk ran willingly enough on continental music, in fact he took no initiative. On the other hand, he spread no embarrassed pools of silence about him and seemed a tranquil part of a friendly atmosphere. This perhaps reflected, from widening experience, what he had earlier, though in a special context, already written to his brother from Trieste in 1906:

Sometimes thinking of Ireland it seems to me I have been unnecessarily harsh. I have reproduced (in *Dubliners* at least) none of the attraction of the city, for I have never felt at my ease in any city since I left it, except Paris. I have not reproduced its ingenuous insularity and its hospitality; the latter virtue, so far as I can see, does not exist elsewhere in Europe.[2]

[1] Harry Levin, *James Joyce* (London, 1944), p. 13.
[2] Herbert Gorman, *James Joyce* (New York, 1939), p. 170.

Ibsen had the same second thoughts: 'The man who has made his home abroad in many foreign countries feels himself never at home in the depths of his soul. Perhaps not even in his own fatherland.'

Dublin was more to Joyce than Norway to Ibsen even though, as Yeats said, 'when driven into exile by, as he thought, his fellow–countrymen Ibsen never forgot the little seaboard towns of Norway'.[1] Joyce wrote in 1902 that the epic poet must keep at a distance from his work. He was following this instinct when he kept Europe between him and his subject. Only from a distance could he modulate the rumour of its streets, set the dream-stage for the dance of its images, and subject its form and history to his kaleidoscopic re-creation.

[1] W. B. Yeats, *Explorations* (London, 1962), p. 161.

4

Joyce in Paris

WARS at home and abroad intervening, I saw nothing of Joyce from 1909 until 1921. He had come to Paris from Zürich in 1920 and, I being in France in the autumn of 1921, we arranged a meeting. Our rendezvous was on the Pont des Arts under the shadow of the Institut and I went there with a picture forming in my mind of a meeting years before on the Blacquiere Canal Bridge in Dublin and of the changes the troubled years must have wrought in his appearance. Knowing enough of the hard struggle he had had in Trieste and Italy and of the glaucoma with which he was afflicted, I expected a ravaged apparition. I was therefore gladly surprised at the elegant figure which alighted from a taxi. A slight moustache and beard accentuating the lines of his face were new to me; his eyes were shaded with powerful lenses; but his carriage was brisk and his debonair carrying of a cane diverted one's attention from his defective sight. Of that afternoon as of all our later meetings I have the friendliest recollections but, from the point of view of literature, recollections of little worth, for Joyce preferred to gossip about Dublin than talk literature. We went to lunch, at my suggestion, to a restaurant near the Luxembourg—*not* Foyot's. I was only gradually to level up my awareness of Joyce's choice in the matter of food. Never gourmand, considerations of health made him here as selective as in all things. But, anyway, we ate oysters and I answered all his questions about Dublin and his Dublin acquaintances and realized how he loved to reconstruct its streets in the precise succession of shops, houses, and their occupants. The only flaw I could find in his rebuilding was his omission of the recent asphalting of the streets and the increasing smell of petrol. There was no trace left in his speech of his former abrupt silences, no needless reticence, but a quiet gravity and some courteous reserve. He told me, however, of Miss Weaver's princely generosity and his freedom from financial worry. He liked Paris as a place to work in, a place where you could be and let be; Nora and his family liked it better than his own possible preference for some place nearer the Mediterranean. On a later occasion he was more explicit and emphasized the debt he was under to the generous recognition extended to him by French writers in Paris. This I was to see for myself.

Joyce had been sending me copies of the *Little Review* and the *Egoist* in which episodes from *Ulysses* had been appearing since 1918. After lunch we crossed over to the Café d'Harcourt and talked of the completed work which was to be published in the following spring.

I made it evident that, however much I appreciated the sections I had read, I had formed no idea of the Homeric framework and had only a rough notion of many of the secondary associations. Such lapses of intelligence happen when a strange planet swims into the literary firmament. Nor did I carry every detail of the *Odyssey* in my head. No Grecian, I had read, like Joyce, Lamb's *Adventures of Ulysses* at school and in later years, with less attention, I had read Butcher and Lang's at one time esteemed translation. Joyce was at pains to take me step by step through all the wanderings of Bloom and Dedalus, plotting out the Homeric parallels, courteously but quite erroneously assuming that I knew every splinter from the *Wandering Rocks* and that I had not failed to observe and remember the meshing of every cog in his mechanism of time and space.This patient courtesy was characteristic of him but it was also deliberate. I was presently to see in print the evidence of similar conversations and like instruction. Joyce was a serious artist. When writing, he thought of his work only. He made no concessions in the interests of easy and immediate communication. But, when his work was finished, he treated it objectively and did not underestimate the necessity of smoothing its path to ultimate intelligibility. When I had heard him out, I said tritely that this Homeric scaffolding was no doubt helpful to him in composition but mattered little when the building was up. He seemed to agree, but I felt his assent was no more than a politeness. I began to think as I think now that these and similar parallels and correspondences had begun to be of great importance to him. They lay at the foundation of Joyce's experimental and characteristic work where time is expanded or folded up like a concertina with the same overlapping of planes and with metamorphoses or liquefaction of objects. In his own art Braque was making not dissimilar experiments in space control in the series of *Ateliers* on which he was working off and on from 1939 to 1954.[1]

I recall only one other instance of any sustained conversation on the work he was engaged on. It was five years later in his apartment, and we were discussing a section of *Work in Progress* which had appeared in the *Criterion*. Again I could not conceal my far greater bafflement at a form as strange as that by which old Jacopone da Todi *nova mundum arte delusit*. Like everyone else I wanted to know why he was doing it. His reply was succinct: it was a night-piece and the language of night is not the language of day. Had Paul Valéry written a letter which in fact he did not write until a year later, Joyce might at this point have invoked it as an authority for Earwicker's prolonged dream and indeed for Molly Bloom's monologue:

Figurez-vous que l'on s'éveille au milieu de la nuit, et que toute la vie se revive et se parle à soi-même. .... Sensualité, souvenirs, émotions, sentiment de son corps, profondeur de la mémoire et lumières ou cieux antérieurs révus etc. Cette trame qui n'a ni commencement ni fin, mais des nœuds, —j'en ai fait un monologue auquel j'avais imposé, avant de l'entreprendre, des conditions de forme aussi sévères que je laissais au fond de liberté.

Settling down to closer discussion, he tried to make clear to me its polymorphism—the transmogrifications by which his figures, animate or inanimate, obscure or famous, *urbi et orbi*, were liable to sudden change, dissolving and re-forming themselves in Earwicker's dream at any point of time.

He set out for me H. C. Earwicker's omnipresent role, but he did not tell me of something I dropped on much later in a collection of sketches by the Victorian caricaturist, Harry Furniss.[3] These caricatures from Mr. Gladstone's days include one of H. C. E. Childers (p. 44). It has the caption 'H. C. E. Childers' with the sub-title 'H(ere) C(omes) E(verybody) CH–LD–RS'. The sketch is of a small-ish, stout figure, strutting forward importantly—as well he might if he knew himself the eponymous ancestor of the Finnegans.

But Joyce did on that earlier occasion introduce me to the *Scienza Nuova* and Vico's theory of history, pointing out its relation with

---

[1] Braque's *Ateliers;* and John Richardson on Braque in the *Burlington Magazine*, June 1955. I find the analogies irresistible.

[2] Quoted in G. Brereton, *Introduction to the French Poets* (London, 1956), p. 263.

[3] *M.P.s in Session 1882–1890, Five hundred sketches of eminent members of the House of Commons 1882—1890* (London, n.d.).

his own *Work in Progress*. Before I left he took down and lent me Michelet's translation of the *Scienza Nuova*, directing my attention to the passage in the introduction which begins:

Le malheur c'est qu'arrivé là, il se trouvait seul: personne ne pouvait plus comprendre. L'originalité des idées, l'étrangeté de langage l'isolait également. Généralisant ses généralités, formulant, concentrant ses formules il employait les dernières comme locutions connues. Il lui était arrivé le contraire des Sept Dormants. Il avait oublié la langue du passé et ne savait plus parler que celle de l'avenir. Mais si c'était alors trop tôt aujourd'hui peut-être c'est déjà bien tard. Pour ce grand et malheureux génie le temps n'est jamais venu. . . . Malgré l'obscurité qui en résulte, malgré l'emploi continuel d'une terminologie bizarre que l'auteur néglige souvent d'expliquer, il y a dans l'ensemble du système présenté de cette manière, une grandeur imposante et une sombre poésie qui fait penser à celle de Dante.

La science nouvelle puise à deux sources: la philisophie, la philologie. La philosophie contemple le vrai par la raison; la philologie observe le réel, c'est la science des faits et des langues.

The passage continues after the enumeration of those fundamental principles which Tacitus calls *foedera generis humani* to Vico's classification of the three ages of human society which Joyce adopts, the divine or theocratic, the heroic, the human or civilized. These pages from Michelet's introduction to his translation of the *Scienza Nuova* bear closely on the plan, structure, and language of *Finnegans Wake*.

I had hardly got back to our hotel when a packet arrived from Joyce, and I turned from Michelet to my first reading of *Anna Livia Plurabelle* in the October 1925 issue of *Le Navire d'Argent*. For its better understanding I found myself reading it aloud to my wife. Turning over a page I dropped on this note written on thin paper which he had enclosed: 'You may wish to have A. (Anna) before the corrected version appears in the October *transition*. The piece should be read half aloud, without a break and rather rapidly. J. J.', and with these two keys I had to unlock its secrets before rejoining the Joyces for dinner at Les Deux Trianons. The time and place, however, and the necessity to introduce my daughter, not yet in her teens, to a dish of frogs, excluded further exegesis. Many years before, Dr. Sigerson had introduced me to these delicate morsels at the Café Véfour. Such traditions had to be maintained and passed on while Anna Livia flows. But before the evening was out Joyce did tell me—as no doubt he told others—that when he had finished the Anna Livia episode

his heart was filled with misgivings. He went down that evening to
the Seine and listened near one of its bridges to its waters:

> . . . sans cesse vagabonde
> Caquetant pur ton gravois
> D'une floflottante voix.

He came back, he said, content.

Joyce was not a table-talker. With me, as I have said, his talk was
of Dublin all the time, Dublin, old and new, with every possible
picturesque revival of its familiar figures of the eighties and nineties
out of our own and our fathers' time. In such exhumations he could
be extraordinarily entertaining. At other times, with strangers present, you became one of a secret society. A party to his grotesque
invention, these intricate leg-pulls which he would conduct with
enormous gravity now seem a farcical shadow-play anticipating
Finnegans Wake. His talk never ran on books and, as much from
disinclination as from his failing sight, he seemed to read little of
his contemporaries. He listened more than he spoke. He was insati-
able for fresh local and personal details, question following question,
the answers being turned over and collated carefully and critically in
his mind and filed as it were for future reference, before giving place
to further queries. As if still 'divining intrigue', there was the usual
slight but noticeable interval between what you said and his next
question. There was no scrap of malicious talk—ever since I knew
him he scorned such gossip—but he took a real and undisguised
interest in people's attitude and behaviour and in the fortunes of his
acquaintances. There was nothing intrusive in his inquisition. It ran
along with caustic appreciation and much spirited burlesque and came,
plainly, from his determination to keep the picture of his town clear
and firmly established in his mind. He loved best to talk of singing
and the theatre but did not disdain discussion of food and drink in
different countries and liked to classify his friends' tastes in such
minutiae. In all his conversation he was simple and unaffected,
obtruding none of his preferences intolerantly, but while speaking
clearly on many matters that touched himself personally he would
not go beyond an obviously predetermined point in regard to the
progress or process of his own creative work. He never entered with
me on his profounder beliefs, but showed an equally studied consideration for those of his friends. Throughout all this later period I
found no embarrassment but only great and watchful courtesy; even

when at a distance and at his blackest hours some twist of wry
humour would appear, making the strain tolerable. In company his
high spirits abounded, but neither then nor at any time in my recollection was there any bawdy in his talk—Sancho Panza and Don
Quixote in plenty but Panurge never and Pantagruel only on the
satiric side. When we met in Paris on later occasions he was increasingly preoccupied with his daughter's illness and his mind was never
free from the dread of war and further dislocation. He shrank from
all violence and with a sort of stoic passivity watched the terrors
gathering in the dark. Yet, in front of this fatalism, his interest in
life was so vivid and the pleasure he took in his friends and family
circle, and most of all in his wife's challenging and gay intelligence,
so engrossing that my Paris memories of him are most exhilarating.
They are associated with afternoons in apartments which were never
the same—the Joyces seemed perpetually to be changing or about to
change their flat—and with evenings at the Deux Trianons, the
Taverne de l'Alsace, Chez Francis, and Fouquet's. But there was
nothing memorable in such meetings other than the evidence of
friendship.

One supper party at Fouquet's remains in my mind because we had
Marlene Dietrich as our nearest neighbour. Fouquet's was a then
fashionable resort of theatrical and cinema stars. Going there one
evening from his flat, whether of malice aforethought or not, Joyce
conveniently forgot a book he wished to give me and so—sending
our wives ahead—Joyce with Eugène Jolas and myself went back
to fetch it and, ignoring warnings given us, we interposed an
interval *en route* for pernods. Warned I suppose by the earlier
arrival of our wives, there was a great to-do when we made our
appearance. Piccolo and commissionaire were strung out on the
pavement. Piccolo signalled commissionaire, commissionaire passed
the signal to the *maître d'hôtel* advancing from the doorstep. I
almost saw a red carpet. Commissionaire took and handed Joyce
back his cane, piccolo took and passed on hats and coats, and the
maître d'hôtel, preceded by the piccolo carrying my two-volume
Lasteyrie, which I did not choose to lose sight of, led us in procession
to what I suppose was Joyce's accustomed place. I found Nora pointing out the celebrities to my wife as they arrived, both forgetful of
reproaches in their anxiety not to miss Marlene's usual moment of
arrival. But the manner of our entry was a challenge—hers was no
more distinguished—and when she did arrive I kept my attention

fixed on Joyce and our conversation and for the rest of the evening did not remove my eyes from his. I imagine that Nora did not fail to appreciate my sense of values. At any rate the pernods were forgiven.

I remember only the gaiety of those evenings and recollection of them is now mingled with my daughter's account of similar later meetings when she was working in Jeanne Bucher's gallery in Montparnasse and seeing the Joyces each week. Joyce loved the theatre, whether it was opera or Jules Verne at the Châtelet to which he took my wife, or the Odéon to which he took my daughter to see *L'Abbé Constantin* in honour of her father's name. I missed all such occasions but more greatly regret absence from his birthday celebrations, honoured each year in set form, Joyce wearing an ancestral waistcoat in brocade and at a given moment executing his ritual dance, a special slip-jig. In one of these, however, which was attended by my daughter I took part from a distance. It was in 1938 and was notable for us inasmuch as Radio Eireann signalized it with a Joyce programme in which I took part. Joyce, as I have already said, attached high importance to any family occasion and this time there was more than usual fuss. Preparatory letters and telegrams were vigorously interchanged between us, and exact synchronization of time established with New York and Mitteleuropa, wherever a Joyce might be at the moment. The evening when it came was divided into two parts: one at the Joyce flat to hear the broadcast, and the second for dinner at the Jolas's, but perhaps I had better with some discretion quote from a letter written to me by my daughter at four o'clock in the morning on her return from the dinner:

We heard the broadcast at the flat with Sam Beckett and an Italo-Swiss music and art critic from Zürich. Joyce fussed around there for some time inspecting the presents and wires and finally proceeded after violent argument over the lost record of Yvonne Printemps to the Jolas's in a taxi full of bottles of wine and cheese, crackers and records and us, of course, singing. At the party were the Gormans, John—greatest-singer-in-the-world—Sullivan, pompous but amusing, the Pelorsons, Paul Léon and Peggy Guggenheim. . . . Dinner was aided and abetted by a fascinating Russian waiter called Conrad. There was a big cake in the middle in green and white with THE BOOK and the Liffey *et tous* raised on it and 56 candles. We ate that with champagne after dinner and lots and lots of Alsatian wine. I remember . . . Claire Gorman shrieking about Beethoven and . . . Léon yelling at me trying to persuade me that Whistler was a Russian . . . and guessing games about the title of W.I.P. only known to Mrs. Joyce—a secret which she has kept sixteen years and did not propose to keep a minute longer; but she was silenced and we took to pulling crackers and then we all with hats on went inside to the salon. First there was Giorgio (who was then in New York) singing on the gramophone and then the piano got going and whiskey and brandy flowed and Philippe Soupault came in and Joyce sang from *Ulysses* and come-all-ye's and *Siubhail a rúin* and then Mrs. Jolas and Sullivan together—he should not be let do it within a radius of 50 yards—and then Joyce sang *Phil the Fluther* and danced and pretty well went on dancing until after three. I talked to everybody far too much, and had a grand time. . . . Mrs. Joyce is thrilled that the broadcast happened in Dublin. Everybody loves Daddy's little moustache and reckons Joyce will be put on the map in Ireland. Finally we got away out on to the rue Borghese, Joyce capering along on Léon's arm still with a yellow hat on while Conrad went chasing ahead for a taxi. Seven of us got in and we saw the last of the *Geburtstagskind* singing on his own doorstep. After that Beckett and the rest of us went and had fruit drinks to sleep on. We were all pretty jaded . . . but the plumpudding came just at the right moment. . . . It is nice to hear of people quietly planting sub-hirtilla but of course Europe is one thing, Ireland another. Now I'm going to bed for a change.

Joyce was ever at pains to study his friends' tastes and to serve them. His anxiety to give them pleasure and his sense of hospitality were so embarrassing to me that at times I had to keep him in the dark as to my own holiday movements so as not to disarrange unduly his own plans and mine. When we did meet there was no gainsaying him. You were body and soul at his disposal. He had a planning mind and your days were blue-printed for you. At home in Dublin I was amused to find this servitude in a more distinguished instance than my own. On a May afternoon in 1937 at the Courts I had a telephone message from my wife to say that a French academician, whose name was unfamiliar to her, was calling that evening to our house and that I should be prepared to meet him. It appeared that Louis Gillet, editor of the *Revue des deux mondes*, member and perpetual secretary of the French Academy, son-in-law of René Dominic, brother-in-law of Henri de Régnier, nephew of the late (the more than late, Joyce said) José-Maria de Hérédia, had somewhat unexpectedly arrived that morning and was met by his hosts of the French Legation and by Professor Roger Chauviré. Chauviré had just rung up my wife to tell her that Gillet's first inquiry at Dun Laoghaire pier was as to my whereabouts. He wished to meet me. That could easily be arranged, Chauviré said, as the day was Wednesday, when we kept open house for our friends. When he arrived, Gillet told me he was a friend of Joyce who wished him to call on us. Before we separated that evening, I tried to arrange for some excursions with him during his stay. He knew Dublin from at least one previous visit. Should we not therefore drive through the mountains and see Glendalough? Chauviré supported me, but Gillet in his slow, deep voice murmured something about rhododendrons in Howth. Were they not now in bloom? We said they were but Glendalough was a famous site and more worth seeing. Gillet said he understood that the rhododendrons in Howth made a very pretty sight. We said they certainly did but that Glendalough had a spectacular situation in the mountains, a sanctuary with historical and architectural associations going back from the thirteenth to the sixth century. Gillet said he would like to see the rhododendrons. We left it at that for the moment. Armed with maps, we met for lunch next afternoon at Jammets and renewed our proposals but, finding him still obdurate, to Howth we went. We were sitting at the foot of the rhododendron cliffs admiring their blaze of colour when I suddenly remembered that on leaving my house that morning I had got a letter from Joyce which I had put, unread, in my pocket, his handwriting requiring some quiet attention. I took it out now to read it and found that it was to announce Gillet's visit; it made also a quite casual allusion to the rhododendrons which should be blooming in Howth. So Gillet's obstinacy was explained. Joyce had blue-printed his programme. Gillet had obviously received his instructions that he was to report on the rhododendrons and he had to obey.

Louis Gillet, whose facial appearance was not unlike that of the sculptured Christ on the Romanesque tympanum at Moissac, had a wide and deep knowledge of European art and literature. The generosity of his intellect had brought him close to Joyce in an intimacy which was none the less valued because he possessed a fine bass voice and had at one time trained for a musical career. He has left his own memorial of friendship in his *Stèle pour James Joyce* (Marseilles, 1941) and in the introduction he wrote for the edition of *Chaucer's A.B.C.* which was decorated by Lucia Joyce. That edition was indeed made at his prompting. The poem had its origin in an address to the Blessed Virgin written by the Prior of the Cistercian Abbey of Châlis, and what still stands of that thirteenth-century foundation had become Gillet's home, more loved than his apartment in the Rue Bonaparte. Lying in the midst of the forests of the Île de France, amid ponds that drank the moonlight—his own description— my wife, daughter, and I were his guests there and learned to appreciate his generous culture and his friendship for the Irish writer whose work he vindicated against the open hostility and more shabby intrigues of Sir Edmund Gosse. In my copy of Lucia Joyce's work I am proud to have my own name linked with his in his inscription of it: *Tibi Constantino Jacobi amico ego Jacobi amicus Louis Gillet.*

Bereft of medical attention, Gillet died in hardship in 1943 in unoccupied France, a victim of the Nazis. In that, he was only a little less unfortunate than Paul Léon who was last seen half-carried by his companions in misery in a wretched procession to a concentration camp. Léon, with whom I had much correspondence, was a lawyer and sociologist interested in international jurisprudence and most unselfishly devoted to Joyce, transacting for him all his business. My last days with Joyce and Nora were spent part in his company at Fontainebleau, driving in the forest, eating *sucre d'orge des réligieuses* at Moret, loafing happily in the sun in quiet ripples of chaff and reminiscence.

In between these rare meetings, from the time Joyce left Dublin, we had maintained a dropping correspondence. Quick interchanges alternated with long silences, but contact was never broken. Not many letters passed between us when he lived at Trieste but he sent me an article or two from those he wrote for the *Piccolo della Sera* such as 'L'Ultimo Feniano', written in 1907 on the death of John O'Leary. I seem to remember one such article—or was it only a conversation—that described an entertaining encounter which Joyce had when he took a *carrozza* outside Milan, at Gorgonzola, with the intention of driving in it to Venice. The horse was recalcitrant, it shied at all uniforms, including, most inconveniently, all policemen. Joyce gradually learned its history. It began its adult career as a Dublin tram horse; was sent out with the Dublin Fusiliers to the Boer War; miraculously escaped the attention of De Wet, and now was ending its days in Lombardy. And its name, believe it or not, was Dublino. But perhaps this story only existed in a conversation!

His books came to me with brief notes as they appeared. But the surviving letters are few. I find I have no more than thirty, a slender garner for a series that began in 1904 and ended in 1940 when growing blindness forced him to supplement our correspondence with messages from Paul Léon. Those that remain are therefore discontinuous. Furthermore, though they are never without a vivid mordant phrase, and their own unmistakable character, few bear directly enough on his work to make them part of literary history. There is no abstract discussion of literary criticism and there are no passages of set description. They are direct and practical, humorous, scathing, or preoccupied with some anxiety. Joyce was no more a letter-writer than a table-talker, and these letters were certainly not written with any idea of ultimate publication. They turned, for the most part, on his family affairs or on some immediate business with such exchanges and inquiries as pass between friends at a distance. Of those I have, a sad number were written in distress of mind during crises of illness in his family and are poignant memorials of his affection for his father and children. In spite of any early repudiation of 'castellar rights' he remained closely knit in spirit with his father. His family, however scattered, was an ever-present concern with him; himself thoroughly domesticated, he kept his correspondent in touch with his family affairs and, just as he welcomed every recognition of a domestic occasion, he was also punctilious and mindful with regard to his friends' domesticities.

In a letter of 1937 he recalls that at Clongowes Father Conmee used to say that his letters home were like grocers' lists and confesses *sono sempre quello*. He was right except that now his demands were prepaid—Joyce was very scrupulous in transactions involving money. But his requirements were numerous and *recherché* and not the easier to meet when the neat handwriting of his early days became more difficult to decipher. I sent him once a long list of theatrical engagements from a file of Dublin eighteenth-century newspapers only to find that what was requested was, more reasonably, from the nineteenth century. On another occasion I was almost misled into a rendezvous with him at Paramé instead of Paname.[1] The requests were diverse. One was for Irish poplin of a certain colour to make book-markers or to decorate a book for Nora. Others, and they were plentiful, were for pantomime librettos, music-hall songs, etc., and their yield is submerged in *Finnegans Wake*. From many he wanted the music more than the words, for his own singing and as a keepsake for his son Giorgio. These sent me ransacking music shops in Capel Street and along the quays for the songs of Ashcroft, Wheatley, Val Vousden the elder, and Percy French.

[1] Paname—slang name for Paris, deriving from the Panama Canal scandal.

Alone amongst these, Percy French's songs are still on the air. His name alone is written in the stone and water of a public memorial. The others are recorded in a more obscure and more lasting monument. The moralizing type of Val Vousden's entertainments is now long out of date, entertainments in which songs such as 'Let Each Man Learn to Know Himself' were interspersed with dancing in a variety of character-sketches ingeniously linked to make one-man shows—*The Unity of Nations* and *The Rosicrucians*. In these productions in the Antient Concert Rooms, words, music, dialogue, and dancing were all his own work and—unless for reasons well-known to his audience and not unexpected—his performance was exemplary in its smooth elegance. He lived to a fine age. Joyce knew Vousden and his songs and it is regrettable that the last he saw of him was, he wrote, when he was making a patriarchal entry into the Black Maria outside Store Street police station. He had a long white beard, typifying, he said, the wisdom of the morning after. In earlier years, in his morning glory, by an advertisement in the next day's papers the entertainer would excuse his failure to appear on the stage, pleading an accident to his ankle.

Horace Wheatley was a nearer contemporary of ours and was to be seen at the Gaiety and Queen's Theatre pantomimes throughout the nineties. The indispensable Widow Twankey and watchful mother of all our Christmas heroines, his gags and songs like 'Morgan the Hatter' were clearly localized and informative. Ashcroft, The Solid Man, reigned a little earlier in our music-halls. He had graduated at the Grafton Theatre of Varieties in South Anne Street. His reputation was established in the eighties; his songs, however, were sung in our period. One of Joyce's particular requests to me was for his famous 'A Quarter to Two' and I can now guess the reason, since the victim of the inaccurate timekeeper in that song was of the same avocation as the eponymous hero of *Finnegans Wake*.

> She wakes me up in the morning,
> Calling the hour of six,
> I'd the deuce of a race,
> To get to the place
> For work of carrying bricks.

The family 'flitting' is still remembered:

> McGovern carried the crockery ware,
> The cradle was handed to me,

Murphy sat on the top of the cart,
Houldin' the clock on his knee.
The horse set off at a funeral trot, etc.

Another letter mentions James Gunn of the Gaiety, a good friend
of Joyce's father's, and another friend, R. J. Thornton, told him of
Guiglini who sang with Tietjens here in 1857 and flew his big kite on
Sandymount strand when he was a boy. Dubliners, he said, ranked
Guiglini, as a tenor, above Mario. Joyce, however, did not mention
that, favourite though Guiglini was with Dubliners, he suffered once
at their hands. Piccolomini had made his farewell appearance with
the company in 1858 and was escorted in a torchlight procession
from the Gaiety to the Gresham. Guiglini was with him and had to
address the demonstrators at Nelson Pillar. 'I thank and love you'
was all he could say in English. His love was diminished when he
discovered his watch had been lifted in the crowd.

His father's friendship with the Gunns continued in the second
generation. Michael Gunn's son, Selskar, used to go to the opera
with the Joyces, and his sister Haidée told him of the many allusions to her father and mother she had seen in *Work in Progress*.
As for myself, I saw Haidée Gunn with Viola Tree make her début in
the Gaiety as a very tall, very charming Juliet. She also appeared in
a scene from *The School for Scandal* playing Lady Teazle, one of her
mother's notable parts. In *Finnegans Wake* the allusions to Haidée's
mother are to her appearances when she was still Bessie Sudlow,
captivating Dublin by her beauty and charm in pantomime. She
excelled also in light Shakespearian parts like Ariel, but it was in
pantomime—as the hero in Edwin Hamilton's *The Yellow Dwarf*
and in *The Babes in the Wood*, but most particularly in *Cinderella*,
that she had Dublin at her feet. She made her last appearance in that
role in 1877, directly after her marriage to Michael Gunn, and her
glorious apparition in ballroom splendour remained long in the
memory of our parents. The aforesaid Edwin Hamilton was unique
in winning the Vice-Chancellor's medal for English verse in Trinity
College by his comic rhymes. He became an assiduous pantomime
librettist and I was enlisted in Joyce's quest for the texts of these
ancient masterpieces—*Turko the Terrible, The Yellow Dwarf, The
Babes in the Wood,* and *Rhampsonitus*. To uncover their rhythms in
Finnegans Wake is the task of thesis hounds. For Joyce they were a
part of his father's estate—voices from a Dublin that was slipping
away and which he would blend with the waters of Anna Livia. Not

easily fobbed off from the completion of his collection, he noted the absence of Val Vousden's 'Let It Pass' and Percy French's 'Andy McElroe' from one of my consignments. Paul Léon sent me other reminders; on one I note an endorsement: Percy French's 'Mulligan Masquerade', Ashcroft's 'Quarter to Two', already mentioned, 'McGinty the Swell of the Sea', 'Mind You That Now', and Vousden's 'Time and Tide'. Paul Léon's letter goes on, 'I have just received from Mr. Joyce a letter and a card where he adds to the list a song the name of which I cannot decipher. I think it is "The Soldier's Song". In case it is unobtainable he would like it to be copied.' Paul Léon, of course, was unaware that the song had become our national anthem. So Joyce spun his web.

At Christmas 1933 I had a letter from him telling me he had asked his friend Antoine Establet who owned a vineyard at Avignon to send me a case of Clos S. Patrice, 1920, *rouge*. It was like him to remember our different taste in the matter of wine and my preference for red burgundy.

I never drink it myself [he wrote] as I dislike red wine but it is really wine from the royal pope. The vineyard is at Chateau-neuf du Pape, the oldest in that part of France and Establet who inherited it says that before the sojourn of the Popes at Avignon the wine of the country was known as *Vin de S. Patrice*. I never met a fellow-islander who had heard of it but I mentioned it to Count O'Kelly, the Irish Free State envoy here and to Dulanty in London and they said they would get it for dinner, etc. There is another S. Patrice below Tours but it is only a *Vin de pichet*.

It was equally like him that having learned the history of this *cru* which had hithero not been particularized other than as Châteauneuf, he should have set himself to revive its original name and to get Establet to issue his product with the old title on specially designed labels indicating its Irish connexion and to secure its appearance on the tables of our legations abroad. At first its issue in the special form was deliberately limited, but the wine is now on general sale under its original name.

A gift of this sort had to be treated with respect and accordingly I produced it only on St. Patrick's Day under *geasa* that my guests should be men of letters worthy of it. My first party included Stephen Gwynn, my elder in vintage lore, and to him it was a novelty. Then, in soaking off and sending him the wine label, I anticipated a request from him. To my surprise, a year or two later, I saw in Charles

Berry's book—I speak of the well-known expert of St. James's Street—a quotation from a letter of mine to Gwynn with reference to another French-Irish vineyard:

I think you and I will agree that this [S. Patrice] vintage should be our national drink at this season and should be admitted to this country free of all duty except that of drinking it. When this objective has been reached it will be our next business to have restored to the Dublin diocese that portion of *Hibernia irredenta* which includes the Archbishop of Dublin's vineyard at Beaune.[1]

Mr. Berry also noted that in 1822 the topographer Jullien mentions the same *cru*, S. Patrice, as 'worthy of being considered of the highest class'.

Next Saint Patrick's Day the poet-philologist Osborn Bergin, most learned of my friends, and the poet-historian Edmund Curtis sat in to our table.[2] The ritual toasts to Saint Patrick and James Joyce having been drunk, our talk turned to folk-songs. Singing by way of illustration kept pace with our meal. A day or two later I met Bergin on the Rathmines bus and he silently fished some Latin verses out of his pocket. They were commemorative of our dinner. I praised them and said they had everybody in them except Petrarch and Vaucluse. As silently he put them back into his pocket, but next evening, stimulated by a hexametrical postcard, I had from him a full version. The lines are a more than sufficient excuse for my long story. Here they are:

> De Vino Patriciano
> *Artificum nutrix multorum et blanda noverca,*
> *qui procul a patria continuere gradum,*
> *Gallia purpureis hoc Narbonensis in uvis*
> *laetificum vinum coxit amoena tuis.*
> *Saepe duo calices juvenem fecere disertum,*
> *et tribus exhaustis concinuere senes*
> *Ipsum hoc Petrarcam redimitum tempora lauro*
> *fontibus arcebat, Sorgia clare, tuis.*
> *Talia Magnorum lenibant pocula curas*

---

[1] c.f. *Crede Mihi*, No. LXV, for the purchase of this vineyard by Henri de Loundres, Archbishop of Dublin.

[2] Curtis had already been celebrated by Bergin in Gaelic verse commemorating their visit by boat to Clonmacnois with Sean Fraser. That was in 1910, *'agus Éamonn geal dár stiúradh'*.

Pontificum, stabat dum furor Urbis atrox.
Dolia deinde pio mercator nomine signat,
Pontificisque nova captat ab arce notam.
Quamvis dulce tamen maturat Avenio vinum,
dulcior a titulo fit meliore sapor.
Felix qui repetens volventibus impiger annis,
restituit priscam, nobilis ille, notam;
Qui tardos gressus cognovit Ulixis Ierni
(quid latet in tumido, Daedale, corde tuo?)
Qui, quo splendidior reddatur debita vino
gloria, 'Patricius tale bibebat' ait.
Advena Patricius colles (quis nescit?) amavit,
qua Rhodanus ridens sole calente ruit.
Tune feres umbram veteris, Provincia, laudis,
immemor et tanti semper amantis eris?
Nunc saltem cyathus venerabile nomen habebit:
Patricianus erit. Prosit, amice, bibe!

Constantinus adest, ruris, laris, urbias amator,
Musarum cultor, dives amicitiis.[1]

There are other allusions in the letters which I should gloss. In September 1929 Joyce refers to a proposed reproduction on the

[1] Or, as translated by my friend, Mr. Niall Montgomery:

Fair France—enchanting foster-mother, nurse of many artists whose foot-steps mingled, far from their native lands, west of the Alps—out of your purple grapes, you made this gladsome wine. Two glasses oft have loosed a young man's tongue—three drained, and old men join in song. Clear-flowing Sorgues, this wine kept from your springs Petrarch himself, his temples bound with laurels. Draughts of it lightened the great pontiffs' cares, as, outside, the city's dreadful frenzy raged. Thenceforth the shipper marks his flagons with the honoured name and pirates a trade-mark from the Pope's new castle. (However sweetly Avignon matures the wine, that nobler style makes it taste sweeter still!) Blest he who active in the rush of years remembered and nobly restored the ancient name, he who knew of the late wanderings of the Irish Ulysses (Say, Daedalus, what lies hidden in your swelling heart?), that the debt to the wine be repaid in greater glory, cries: Of such a vintage Patrick drank! Patrick, in exile, may well have loved those hills, where warmed by the sunlight rolls the smiling Rhône. Can you, then, bear the memory of that ancient praise, Provence, unmindful yet, for ever, of so great a lover? Now at least the wine which bore a revered name in future will be called Patrician. Good luck, my friend; drink up! Here with us is Constantine, lover of heath, hearth, and market-place, learned in the arts and with a wealth of friends.

cover of an instalment of *Work in Progress*: there is a reference, I think, to an *objet trouvé* I sent him about this time. On my way to the Courts I had seen on the quays a wood-carving of the arms of the City of Dublin, painted in gesso. It might have come from the old Tholsel or city council or some guild-hall. Believing it would amuse him, I had it packed and dispatched. Later I saw it in Joyce's rooms together with Jack Yeats's pictures of the Liffey. However, the re-production might have been from a finely engraved early nineteenth-century map I sent him—the course of the Liffey from its source above Lough Bray. Plentiful of place names, it was bound to be received with favour.

In September 1935 Joyce mentioned in a letter his sittings to Seán O'Sullivan, R.H.A., for a drawing. The painter had mentioned he was going to Paris and I arranged with Joyce for a drawing. Seán returned with three from which I made my choice; one of the others is now happily in our National Gallery. Joyce said he had found my friend, as I expected, *très sympathique*, but actually the sitting came at an unfortunate moment. He was suffering badly, as his letter suggests, from a deep-seated malady. The drawings betray evidence of this and show him under a strain.

Finally I would refer to certain passages in the correspondence which run counter to the notion that Joyce had a settled determina-tion never to return to Ireland. In March 1920, writing to Frank Budgen from Trieste, he was speculating on the chances of meeting him in England in the summer, 'Perhaps I too might go to Cornwall and then to Ireland.' It was an ill-judged moment for a visit. Dublin lay under curfew. The armed resistance to England was general, and Lloyd George's Black and Tan terror at its height. It was to this situation that Joyce referred in writing to his aunt in Dublin in 1921: 'If the country had not been turned into a slaughterhouse of course I should have gone there and got what I wanted.' To any question of mine on the topic his reply was the evasive: 'Have I ever left it?' In August 1937 he had been writing to me about a proposed visit of his wife to Galway on family affairs. Nora Joyce had an invincible dislike of sea-travel. 'She has never been able', he said, 'to cross water and she will not even trust herself into one of the *bateaux mouches*. It is a frightful job when we get to the channel on rare occasions.' This time Joyce had some idea of accompanying her at least as far as Holyhead, but 'I am trying to finish my W.I.P. (I work about 16 hours a day it seems to me) and I am not taking any chances

Joyce, Paul Léon, and the author outside the Hotel Savoie, Fontainebleau.

Joyce in 1937, drawn by Seán O'Sullivan, R.H.A.

with my fellow-countrymen if I can help it until that is done, at least. And on the map of their island there is marked very legibly for the moment *Hic sunt Lennones*[1] But, every day, in every way, I am walking along the streets of Dublin and along the strand. And "hearing voices". *Non dico giammai ma non ancora.*'

Letters from my daughter to me in 1938 from Paris show that his friends did not believe that he held to any idea of permanent exile. In the February of that year she gathered from Mrs. Joyce and the Jolas's that a combined trip over was in question, 'But I cannot quite fathom how much is in such talk. At least Mrs. Joyce and Jolas are keen but *Work in Progress* must be finished first.' In June of that same year she wrote me:

Went to the Odeon with Joyce on Thursday—*L'Abbé Constantin* in memory of you. Romantic comedy but he mostly laughed at my stories about Newmarket-on-Fergus.[2] Apparently he has been keeping Mrs. Joyce awake at night ever since laughing. He has started speaking at last about finishing his book which I think is really true this time. Then they are coming to Ireland, but of course will have to be kept up to it. I am given a long list of questions to be worked out in Dublin before he can finish it all the same. More work for the stooges.

I do not think that Dublin for permanent residence would, at any time, have suited Joyce's way of working or way of living. Had he lived, he might have come back for some stay, short or long. But I also believe that, although he was arriving at a juster estimate of the appreciation in which his work was held at home, he felt his pride involved. I see him postponing any return until some public recognition of the position he had won after much hardship was offered. Ibsen may still have been in his mind. Anyway, time passed and the opportunity never came. This 'high, unconsortable one' rests with his life's companion in a grave in Zürich.

[1] The allusion is to an ill-conditioned article in an old number of the *Catholic World* (Canada).

[2] The stories, I understand, related to her experiences when assisting in an archaeological 'dig' in Co. Clare.

PART TWO

5

Joyce's D'Annunzian Mask[1]

REVIEWING the student years we passed together and figuring out to myself the new moulds in which Joyce's ideas and conduct were then forming, I have been for many years convinced that D'Annunzio was one of the mould-makers. Ibsen, like Yeats, was another and his influence has escaped the attention of none who has written on Joyce. But the 'radiant simultaneity' with Ibsen which Joyce so gladly recognized in 1901 extended even before that date to his Italian contemporary and Joyce for some years lay fully in his orbit. None, save his brother, has pointed in this direction and these brief references of Stanislaus Joyce in his *Letteratura* article, significant as they are, travel even further than they may appear to at first sight. D'Annunzio's influence was as early and almost as strong as Ibsen's. Its evidence lay indeed on the surface, plain to anyone with the clue, and while it lasted it was consonant with Ibsen's and was stylistically more apparent. In Joyce's student years when *fin de siècle* masks were still the fashion it was strong enough to lead to deliberate identification and self-dramatization on his part and to affect his personal behaviour as well as his credo and style.

D'Annunzio, whatever his limitation, takes a place in the train of the great nineteenth-century egotists—Byron, Hugo, Wagner. Like Joyce he did, as Arthur Symons suggests, help to shift interest from the 'exterior' novel to the hidden, inner self which 'sits silent through all our conversation'. In 1901 Joyce found him the culmination of the tide that rose with Flaubert and certainly with him a new style was born, a theatrical pastiche and a manner which deeply affected a whole section of Italian society.[2] He saw himself as a 'redemptive'

[1] With grateful acknowledgement to the editor of *Studies*, in which part of this chapter first appeared in Summer 1962.
[2] See Luigi Barzini's article in *Encounter*, January 1956.

writer like Ibsen. With superb mastery of language and magnetic eloquence, however overwrought and feverish, he built up a fictitious stage for the Italian superman's choreographic existence.

Abroad, thanks to Eleonora Duse, D'Annunzio was then perhaps more generally known as a dramatist than as a novelist. Led by his own early interest in the theatre, Joyce's attention was drawn to him in 1899 but he knew him in both fields—as did Symons who found place for D'Annunzio's one symbolical novel, *Le Vergini delle Rocce*, in his collection of literary essays. In May 1900, after the publication of his Ibsen article in the *Fortnightly Review*, Joyce, as we know, crossed to London to see Duse's performance in *La Gioconda* at the Lyceum. I have in my collection of books once owned by Joyce, three by D'Annunzio.

D'Annunzio was little read in the Dublin of those years. His plays and poetry, to say nothing of his novels, came slowly to the shelves of the National Library, though Huneker, in 1890, was writing of him as one who with Ibsen and Hauptmann personified the thoughts of the new generation with its contempt for 'the conventional lies of our civilization'. But not later than 1900 Joyce was defending a novel —plainly by D'Annunzio—in Ghezzi's Italian class in University College (*Stephen Hero*, p. 170). It is evident from this, and from his interest in *La Gioconda*, from his reference to *Il Fuoco* in 'The Day of the Rabblement', from the Leonardo–D'Annuzian epigraph with which it opens, and from what I believe to be D'Annuzian echoes in his paper on James Clarence Mangan in February 1902 that Joyce was following all he could of D'Annunzio's work with special attention. Alone in Dublin, I imagine, he had this admiration. One will, I suspect, search in vain for D'Annunzio's name in *Beltaine* or *Samhain* amongst the Ibsens, Björnsons, Hauptmanns, Sudermanns, Tolstois, Maeterlincks, and Echegarays freely mentioned in these organs of the promoters of the Irish Theatre movement. And this is not surprising, for in spite of Yeats's interest in Arthur Symons's explorations there was as much in D'Annunzio at that stage to repel as to attract our Irish poet. The Yeats of 1900 was occupied with folk-lore and magic and with dreams of a theatre whose personae could step clear of any more tangible nets. He lent an ear to Raftery, the Irish folk poet, rather than to the Italian Renaissance. He had not yet made the journey to Urbino and Byzantium.

The traces of D'Annunzio may, I believe, be discerned in many aspects of the youthful Joyce: in his early artificial attitude and bearing towards his fellows; in the methods of his self-discipline as an apprentice-writer; in his Messianic outlook and in his aesthetic gospel. Let us consider these from old recollection and in the light of *Le Vergini delle Rocce* and *Il Fuoco*.

First as to his personal bearing. Joyce left Belvedere for University College in the autumn of 1898. He was then no more than sixteen years old, exceptionally gifted but in no other way singular. None of his Belvedere school-friends describes any undue, habitual aloofness in him at this time or any detachment from school routine. We have authentic recollections from two of his school fellows. William Fallon told me that as a small boy Joyce made a notable Red Indian in spite of his frail physique. He was by all accounts cool and imperturbable, though he took no part in regular school games. Judge Sheehy has written of his useful initiative in school plays and of his talent for satirical improvisation. On the other hand, as I have mentioned earlier, from 1899 none of his University College friends failed to note aloofness and detachment as a special characteristic. It is true that this reserve appeared in different measure. It affected only in a slight degree his old schoolmates and the one or two acquaintances whom he was making his partial confidants. But reserve there was, although open at times to irruptions of sudden merriment. His detachment took more often the form of studied politeness but it fell little short of arrogance in the eyes of many of his fellow-students and it was not less known as such to the group of writers outside the College—generically known as 'the bards'—whose acquaintance he was making and who were later to be the unflattered recipients of his 'Holy Office'.

This change over from normal companionship to an increasingly defiant, arrogant isolation lasted some four or five years and it began quite suddenly—within the space of a twelve-month. It was, of course, part of that 'enigma of a manner' which Stephen describes himself as constructing in his first year at College (*Stephen Hero*, p. 27). Becoming evident in 1899, it is not unreasonable to look for the origin of this change in his reading in that year. Its progression is the subject matter of the *Portrait of the Artist*, but its form and definition are so curiously forecast in D'Annunzio's *Le Vergini delle Rocce* and the parallels so exactly drawn that, when every allowance is made for experiences common to adolescent genius, one cannot escape finding in this novel a direct influence. Long persuaded of its bearing on Joyce's early writing and opinions, I am confirmed in this by

Stanislaus Joyce's categorical references to its effect on his personal behaviour, building up no less than a life in advance. *Le Vergini delle Rocce* certainly helps to explain the mask he wore in his early years. Joyce at seventeen deliberately modelled himself on D'Annunzio and Ibsen. However incongruous his two exemplars were, they had just enough in common for Joyce to build up out of them or their pages a new personality for himself, unconsortable and scornful of public opinion, and with a settled programme and plan of conduct. Ibsen's moral fibre fixed his intransigence but D'Annunzio's heroes left no less unmistakable traces on his public behaviour.

We turn to *Le Vergini delle Rocce* and to supporting passages from *Il Fuoco*, examining their pages not in full detail—for that in view of D'Annunzio's prodigality of lavish language would require too copious transcription—but summarily and with sufficient particularity.[1]

Le Vergini delle Rocce is a novel indeterminately symbolist and allegorical—calculated therefore to attract Joyce as did Yeats's *Tables of the Law*. It begins, as Symons says, with a discourse and ends as a poem—a description which might, indeed, cover Joyce's whole achievement from his essay on Mangan to *Finnegans Wake*. The discourse occupies the first section. Its race-conscious hero, Claudio, seeks to recreate in himself the mannered and masterful personality of an admired Renaissance ancestor and in a degenerate age he faces the self-imposed task of reanimating the exhausted race of his fellow-countrymen with his antique spirit. Under the tutelage of a Socratic demon and of da Vinci he conducts a self-examination which establishes the framework within which he will fulfil his destiny. His faith is in himself and in aesthetics. He believes in the grand manner, defined by Henry James in this immediate D'Annunzian context as 'the sense of the supremacy of beauty, the supremacy of style and, last not least, of the personal will, manifested for the most part as a cold insolence of attitude'.[2]

[1] I use Agatha Hughes's translation of *Le Vergini delle Rocce : The Virgins of the Rocks* (London, 1899).

[2] Henry James, *Notes on Novelists* (London, 1914), p. 221. In his essay 'Poetry and Tradition', W. B. Yeats wrote, as Mr. Niall Montgomery reminds me: 'In life, courtesy and self-possession, and in the arts style, are the sensible impressions of the free mind, for both arise out of the deliberate shaping of all things, and from never being swept away, whatever the emotion, into confusion and dullness.' This comes closer than cold insolence to Joyce's later attitude.

This virtuoso has learned from Leonardo *se tu sarai solo, tu sarai tutto tuo* and that there can be no greater mastery than of oneself. In 'The Day of the Rabblement' Joyce is equally urgent that the artist should isolate himself; he formulates this as a radical principle of artistic economy and as Stephen Dedalus in *Stephen Hero* he repeats it as a first principle (p. 33). Claudio seeks in silence to lift his life above its circumstances and by his will, by selection and exclusion, to prepare himself for his creative work (*The Virgins of the Rocks*, p. 14). So Stephen 'built a house of silence for himself' (*S.H.*, p. 30). He erects his 'breakwater of order', just as Claudio 'after the inevitable tumult of early youth' raised a barrier 'against the confused and multifold overflow of sensations' (*V.R.*, p. 14). The analogies with Stephen grow as we proceed to passages inculcating 'methods to conduct thy being to attain perfect integrity . . . to concentrate the purest essence of thy spirit, and to reproduce in . . . art the deepest vision of thy universe . . .' (*V.R.*, p. 52). Stephen also 'strove to pierce to the significant heart of everything. He doubled backwards into the past of humanity. . . . He seemed almost to hear the simple cries of fear and joy and wonder which are antecedent to all song. . . . And over all this chaos of history and legend . . . he strove to draw out a line of order, to reduce the abysses of the past to order by a diagram' (*S.H.*, p. 33).

But Claudio also has realized his necessity. He also has learned the benefits of order and the ruled design: 'Day after day I felt my whole nature grow, under the rigorous discipline of meditation, selection, and exclusion . . .' [Its marvellous virtue was], 'that although it drove me to order my inner life with the exactness of a ruled design, it did not dry up the spontaneous springs of emotion and imagination . . .' (*V.R.*, p.28). This passage in which the verbal resemblance with the text of *Stephen Hero* is so close is immediately followed by sentences which recall the flowing forth over Stephen's brain of the verses in the *Portrait of the Artist*: Of a sudden a 'jet of poetry would burst from my inner being, filling my whole soul with music and ineffable freshness, and causing desires and hopes to burn higher in a happy flame' (*V.R.*, p. 28). A further passage seems to me again to reflect the young college student's ambitions in point of discipline and design. It is when Claudio learns 'to seek and discover in my own nature genuine virtues and genuine defects, that I might arrange both in accordance with a premeditated design, striving with patient care to give a seemly appearance to the latter, and to raise the former upwards towards the supreme perfection', excluding 'everything which was discordant with my ruling idea . . ., which could slacken or interrupt the rhythmical development of my thought' (*V.R.*, p. 22).

Such passages from *Le Vergini delle Rocce* appear so similar in language and ordonnance to others in *Stephen Hero* and the *Portrait of the Artist* that I hardly know from which text I transcribe. It is true, of course, that they also depict the experience of many another young poet but the analogies grow close in other particulars. Claudio's Socratic demon counselled him 'to compose and cultivate music'. In our college days, if we were alone together and a piano at hand, Joyce would inevitably drift to the keyboard and into snatches of song and recitative. It was then I heard him first sing to his own music certain lyrics by Yeats. As well as being a 'cultivator of music' Claudio is a poet and a master of style. His demon assures him: 'Thou dost possess the gift of poetry and must study to acquire the science of words.' As an avowed student of Leonardo da Vinci he notes down his 'terse, proud sayings' and is drawn by 'the pithy significance of an incisive axiom'. Are we not here alongside Stephen the word-catcher, the lexical student—in the workshop of young Dedalus, fabricating those definitions and terse, proud sayings which he or his creator will throw down at any interlocutor? D'Annunzio endows Stelio, the hero of *Il Fuoco*, with his own exultant mastery of language. Consciously he tries out his mental agility and the facility of his speech. Like Claudio he is prodigal of quotations drawn from carefully recondite sources and spreads embroidered cloths of didacticism before his audience. He cultivates language at two extremes: one, the concise 'da Vincian epigraph'; the other, evocative of dream, unfolding itself in purest verbal music. These are again conspicuous traits marking Stephen Dedalus. Other passages or sentences in *Il Fuoco* carry to me fainter overtones of Joyce's youth. I do not refer so much to the title 'Epiphany of Fire' borne by Part I of the novel, though his appearance of a favoured word may well have now first caught Joyce's attention. I allude rather to other touches descriptive of Stelio which recall Joyce: his liking, for example, for ceremonial (p. 10[1]), his passion for opera, and more particularly the description of Stelio's voice and Stelio's own account of his public speaking. 'I can speak only', he says, 'about myself. Obliged to speak to my audience only of my dear soul I must speak under the veil of seductive allegory

---

[1] *Il Fuoco* (London, 1899). English trans.

and with the magic of gracious cadences'; and he speaks with 'a clear penetrating voice, icy at the start'. Was this passage present to Joyce's mind when he was preparing his paper on Mangan? I conceive no more concise description of this piece of veiled allegory and semi-autobiography and of Joyce's manner in its delivery.

These stylistic and personal details have drawn me away from Joyce's assumption of that 'cold insolence of attitude', which Henry James finds in D'Annunzio's heroes stemming from their sense of the supremacy of beauty and of the personal will. Claudio, meditating on the counsel of Socrates's demon, learns that

the real duty of a man of worth is to discover in the course of his existence a series of harmonies, varied indeed, but controlled by one dominant motive, and bearing the impress of one style. . . . *In his supreme wisdom the ancient sage made his Ideal* 'the living centre of his being and deduced his own laws from it . . . exercising with calm pride such rights as they permitted him, and separating—he, a citizen of Athens under the tyranny of the Thirty, and under the tyranny of the plebeians— deliberately separating his moral existence from that of the city. (*V.R.,* pp. 15, 16.)

And accordingly Claudio, like Stephen, breaks with God and the State. *Non serviam,* says Stephen; and Claudio says that 'I will be obedient to God only' means 'I will be obedient only to the laws of that genius to which, in order to fulfil my conception of order and beauty, I have subjected my free nature' (*V.R,* p. 16).

Claudio, poet and man of action, conceives himself 'destined to engrave on new tables of stone new laws for the religious guidance of the people' (*V.R.,* p. 29) and, as Stephen would forge in the smithy of his soul the uncreated conscience of his race, so Claudio dreams of 'the iron for the plough which shall furrow afresh an exhausted land' (*V.R.,* p. 25). Meanwhile he is harrowed by the ignominy which surrounds him:

the arrogance of the populace was not so great as the cowardice of those who tolerated and supported it. Living in Rome, as I did, I was witness of the most ignominious breaches of faith . . . which ever dishonoured a sacred spot. . . . Like the overflow of sewers, the flood of base desires was invading the market place and the cross-roads. . . . (*V.R.,* p. 24.)

The 'turbid seething of servile passions' surrounded Rome 'like a river of Tartarus'. The sacred city is populated by a miserable race stricken with leprosy re-iterating their dreary complaint. The ancient Persians, as the ever-fresh Herodotus relates, used to attribute this foul infirmity to offences committed *against the Sun*. And these slavish people had indeed offended against the Sun. A certain number of them, hoping to be cleansed, had bathed in great fonts of piety. . . . But the sight of these was quite as repugnant. (*V.R.*, p. 35.)

He envied the young Garibaldian soldier who had 'ceased to form part of a compact and unanimous band, and assumed an individuality of his own, a singularly warlike aspect, consecrated to a new onward movement' (*V.R.*, p. 26).

The poets, meanwhile, 'have exhausted their store of rhymes in evoking images of other days, in weeping over their own dead illusions . . . . Only some magnificent power armed with ideas more brilliant than past memories could be able to raise its head above the monstrous phantoms. . . .' Again, is it Claudio who speaks—or Joyce in his criticism of Mangan?

Claudio's integrity must at all costs be preserved in this 'Day of the Rabblement' and of *La Bestia Trionfante*:

The gaze of the crowd is worse than a splash of mud, the breath of it is poisonous. Go far off while the sewer discharges itself . . . let not thyself be contaminated by the crowd. Thy hour will come (*V.R.*, p. 53.) [And his demon declares:] Everything that is born and exists around thee is born and exists by reason of the breath of thy will and thy poetry (*V.R.*, p. 150). Defend Beauty! [cries Claudio to the poets] Defend the vision that is within you . . . defend yourselves with all your weapons, even with jests, if such are of more use than invectives. Be careful to sharpen the point of your scorn with the bitterest poison. Let your sarcasm have corrosive strength. . . . Let your frenzied laughter rise to the very heaven when you hear the stablemen of the Great Beast vociferating in the Assembly. . . . Defend the Thought which they threaten, the Beauty which they outrage! A day will come when they will attempt to burn the books, shatter the statues, rip up the canvases. (*V.R.*, pp. 36–37.)

These are some draughts of the heady wine Joyce was drinking in 1900 and such passages—denunciatory or hortatory—from *Le Vergini delle Rocce* can be multiplied. They confirm at every point the attitude Joyce was assuming; the deliberateness of his plan and purpose, his reserve, his aloofness from his fellows and scorn of the rabblement, his faith in an autonomous art controlled only by the laws of his own genius. True that, however defiantly borne, these are the not uncommon insignia of many young artists, but they seem

peculiarly to bear upon Joyce's attitude in the years following 1900
and they are accompanied by enough echoes in Joyce's first writings
and in the *Portrait of the Artist,* to make it difficult or impossible to
exclude an immediate influence. Claudio's *cave, adsum* and his *sub
se omnia* are heard in 'The Day of the Rabblement' and in his paper
on Mangan; and the assurance of Claudio's demon that his 'hour
will come' was hardly absent from Joyce's ear when he prefigures
himself as the minister who 'will not be wanting when his hour
comes. Even now that hour may be standing by the door'. The
parallel already mentioned between the forge in Stephen's smithy and
Claudio's ploughshare is accompanied by another passage in *Il Fuoco*
where the protagonist finds in 'the beating of his own heart . . . the
repercussion of the hammer on the hard anvil where human destiny
is forged'. The Herodotean offenders against the sun are glanced at in
the Mangan paper. In *Ulysses* (Paris, 1922, p. 34) Mr. Deasy reproaches these sinners against the light with darkness in their eyes;
they reappear in the Oxen of the Sun episode and indeed are implicit
everywhere in Joyce. The cunning Ulysses (*V.R.*, p. 40) is not absent,
nor the birds of Daedalus whose screams and wingings fill the souls of
Claudio (*V.R.*, p. 102) and of Stephen (*Portrait of the Artist*, p. 263[1])
with ancestral terrors and exultation; their hawk-cries are finally
heard as night falls over *Anna Livia Plurabelle.* Very assuredly, also,
Joyce fulfilled in due time Claudio's divination of 'the power which
the genius of place can exercise over the responsive soul'.

These promptings find other support in the general character of
D'Annunzio's novels. Meditations taking their departure from some
casual sight or phrase stick in my memory as characteristic of the
Stephen Hero MS., which I was reading in 1903–4, but the resemblance between Joyce's first published work and D'Annunzio can be
more clearly indicated. Arthur Symons finds in D'Annunzio's novels
not so much a plot as the progression of states of mind. The interest
lies in the hidden, inner self which sits silent through all conversation. He finds D'Annunzio the attentive and wholly unreticent
recorder of the primary sensations of pain and pleasure. Beginning
with intent waiting upon sensation, he expands his creature of acute
sensibility into a kind of amoral Renaissance personality.[2] Add
D'Annunzio's ever-present vein of lyricism to this exacerbated

[1] London, 1916.
[2] A. Symons, Introduction to *The Child of Pleasure* (Boston, 1898).

sensibility and to the minute inquisitorial distinctions he observes in the world of the senses, and we seem to be very close to the youthful Joyce and can understand the attraction D'Annunzio had for him.

I do not wish to stretch these analogies too far or to ignore other literary influences which ran parallel with that of D'Annunzio. Blake, for example, was ever on the lips of Yeats and A.E. in those days, and was also a favourite of Joyce. The inquisitorial distinctions just mentioned may have had equal encouragement from Blake, who founded all sublimity on 'minute discrimination' and held that 'to Particularize is the Alone Distinction of Merit'. It matters little or nothing whether it was from D'Annunzio or Yeats or even Huysmans (whom Joyce disparaged) or some other that he borrowed the trick of esoteric discourse, whether he got his word-catching from Ben Jonson or, spurning the rabblement, joined the sleeve of communication with D'Annunzio, Bruno, or Leonardo, or with old Seneca who said: 'Flee the crowd, flee from a small group, shun even a single companion.' It is enough to say that like sought out like; that D'Annunzio had Joyce's attention when he was writing on Mangan and *Stephen Hero,* and that in those years he wore a D'Annunzian mask. I do not say that reserve was not as innate in him as a wild humour. But enigmatic detachment was more publicly paraded in his college years; the breakwater was breached only in private fun. D'Annunzio remained all his life inhumanly humourless. Joyce's developed work is notably different in this respect from his early writings. Picasso says it takes a long time to grow young. The young artist treads delicately in the sanctuary and only in his maturity is at ease in Sion. So it was with Joyce, who in his first years drew very strict lines in his aesthetics—stricter and more finely drawn than D'Annunzio's—before giving full play later to his natural humour. There was a second difference in their aestheticism. Both were race-conscious. D'Annunzio's passionate *italianità* clad him with a Messianic mission to transform his fellow-countrymen into 'an ideally potent and perfect race'. Preaching first the efficacy of aesthetics, he turned later to air-bombing. Joyce found the writing of books more life-enriching. When all were thinking of national resurgence, he abstained from any political manifestations. Then and always. But those are gravely mistaken who think him un-Irish or anti-Irish because he quarrelled with one or other expression of a general feeling. He was primarily European but his Irish attitude is significantly enough expressed in a letter written about 1906: 'If the

Irish programme did not insist on the Irish language I suppose I could call myself a nationalist.' He placed a faith greater than D'Annunzio's in aesthetics and grounded thereon his prophecy for the future of his race. To the end he was content to observe Leonardo's epigraph cited in *Le Vergini delle Rocce*: '*Io farò una finzione che significherà cose grandi.*'

6

Ibsen and Others

ITALY is not more different from Norway than D'Annunzio from Ibsen. It approaches a paradox, therefore, to say that Joyce modelled his behaviour on both writers. It is more correct to find the root of Joyce's intransigence in Ibsen's moral fibre and to find his D'Annunzian affinities associated only with certain early attitudes and literary echoes. Ibsen was the earlier and more enduring model and we do not need Joyce's own confession of 'radiant simultaneity' to be persuaded of a more than merely literary influence. This is so plainly understood that I shall refer here only to a detail or two which might have struck Joyce with some special sharpness in the course of his reading of the Scandinavians in 1899 and the years immediately after.

This reading pivoted, no doubt, on the dominant figure of Ibsen but was not confined to him. It covered Brandes extensively; Björnson, who also was to his hand in translations, entered into it; also Jacobsen, whom he introduced in 1901 into 'The Day of the Rabblement'. That reference, it is true, was no more than might have been derived from an encyclopedia article, but Joyce's Danish was something more than rudimentary and the particular contribution which Jacobsen made to Danish literature was such as to arouse his special interest. Joyce, at any rate, was fully conversant with the Danish literary movement from the 1880s. By and large, it was a break-away from conservatism and an inbred self-sufficiency into the fuller currents of European experience and experiment. With Brandes in its critical vanguard, it was a compound of naturalism, symbolism, and satire, and its expression was as much through the novel as the drama. Jacobsen looks askance upon Brandes's programme 'which would make literature a floor for socio-political debate', but 'fulfilled his demands for a psychological novel'.[1]

It is to this fulfilment that Joyce alludes in 'The Day of the Rabblement' when he places Jacobsen between Flaubert and D'Annunzio in the development of the pyschological novel, which goes along with his abstention from political and social problems as matter not befitting the artist. Jacobsen was, furthermore, 'a stylist, a word magician . . . and achieved unusual effects by his handling of paragraph and sentence structure. Long descriptive sentences are broken off by curt momentous remarks'.[2] Such abrupt transitions from reverie and a subjective intricacy to external reality are, as I have said earlier, perhaps my clearest recollection of my reading of the MS. of *Stephen Hero*.[3]

To revert now to Ibsen, Georg Brandes had published his *Ibsen and Björnson* in 1899. Joyce would certainly have read the copy in the National Library when he was preparing his paper 'Drama and Life'. He would have found in its pages the story of a young writer living with a bankrupt father in a home which was beginning to have no great attraction for him. Stephen Dedalus also found it in him to refer to the unpleasant character of his home. Ibsen was entering a literary arena which had many resemblances with the Dublin scene. He was sharing in the activity of the Norwegian theatre—a part, like the Irish Theatre movement, of a general, national resurgence. He found himself fighting on two fronts. The Norwegian stage was beginning to supplant the ascendancy of Denmark and its conservatism. Its writers were pledged to two loyalties: the cult of Norse sagas, and the cult of the Norse peasant. Ibsen's allegiance was given to neither. He used, to be sure, saga material but his modern treatment of these consecrated national themes was only less shocking to the public than his disrespect for the peasant ideal. The public thought him envenomed and he found himself, as Brandes says, continually at war with his countrymen. His first lyrical mood passed over into satire and critical detachment. 'I had not', he himself wrote later, 'the gifts that go to make a good citizen nor yet the gift of orthodoxy and what I possess no gift for, I keep out of.' For this

---

[1] P. M. Mitchell, *History of Danish Literature* (Copenhagen, 1957).

[2] ibid.

[3] I am not competent to say whether or not Jacobsen's *Maria Grubbe* left any traces on Joyce's *Dubliners*. Its sub-title, *Interiors*, and still-life detail as described by Mr. Mitchell may have been in his mind when he turned to the short story but such resemblances, if they exist, had become common property. Flaubert and George Moore were exemplars closer to hand.

isolation Ibsen makes Dr. Stockman, enemy of the people, his mouthpiece who declares the strongest man to be he who stands alone. The real enemies were 'surrender to the trolls and the spirit of compromise'—the spirit which reappears in *Peer Gynt* in the form of the *Boyg*, 'embodiment of all that is cowardly and yielding in man'.[1] Even in the desert he would still preach and not abandon his ambition 'to awaken his people and teach it to think big', but, reduced by poverty and unimpressed by or unwilling to meet the demands of his elders for support (I still quote Brandes), this 'full-blooded egotist' retired abroad to fulfil his mission from a distance. From abroad he retorted fiercely to the critics of his *League of Youth* that 'he had studied the ways and manners of their pernicious and lie-steeped cliques'. As Falk in *Love's Comedy*, or as he shows himself in the bitter lines of his 'Millennial Ode', he took up the staff and weeds of the exile:

> My people gave me the exile's staff,
> The badge of care, the wanderer's shoe of pain,
> The pilgrim's shirt with hardship over-wrought. . .

and remained in self-exile for twenty-seven years.

Joyce was certainly in Ibsen's forge when he was writing 'Drama and Life' in 1899 and watching the development of the Irish Literary Theatre. I do not find it accidental that Ibsen's lines 'To the Poet, H. O. Blom', from which a quotation is made in that paper, echo clearly in Joyce's paper on Mangan as well as in some of his later writing. This poetical epistle to a poet whose name rings another bell is a racy and vigorous repudiation of Blom's lament that with the retirement of a certain conservative Danish actor the end of a Danish tradition meant the ruin of the Norwegian stage. C. H. Herford's adaptation in *Beltaine* runs: 'Never fear, the twilight of the gods will come to an end, a new day is dawning behind yonder hill; and you shall yet see that the daylight can burn the rotten lumber of the past; you shall yet see that beyond the ruined Valhalla rises the new Heaven.'

Herford's quotation is from the last stanza of Ibsen's poem—not, as he says, from the first. To judge its purpose, one should consider the parable in the poem's sixth stanza. The poet sees an embalmed corpse emerging from the shades of the pyramids. Pride is on its strong face and a disdainful smile; long unconscious of the sun's

---

[1] *Ibsen and Björnson.*

majesty, knowing nothing of life's intoxication, it still worships age-old, bankrupt powers; the mummy-mouth smiles scornfully because time will not stand still.

I believe Joyce had this vision before him when he finds Mangan —however admirable a poet, and matchless at times—ultimately the type of his race enclosed so straitly in history that even his fiery moments do not set him free from it. The fair flowers in the queen's garden have become the husks of history and food for boars. A more eager spirit would cast down with violence the high traditions of his race which Mangan has too passively accepted. The vision was still before his eyes when, reviewing Lady Gregory's *Poets and Dreamers* in 1903, Joyce renewed his assault, quite in the Ibsen vein, on the effete traditions of 'feeble and sleepy' minds. The same vision from Ibsen's last stanza holds its place in the closing paragraphs of the Mangan paper. Dusk veils the train of the gods and he who listens may hear their footsteps leaving the world but, though there is dusk about their feet and darkness in their indifferent eyes, the miracle of light is renewed eternally. A new, serene spirit, entering cities and the hearts of men, will sing the glad, underlying life of the earth.

> As you shall yet see, highest of all the heavens
> Is not Valhalla—it is the dawning Gimli

Passing from the assault on tradition, Georg Brandes tempts me to mention one other dominant theme common to Ibsen and Joyce. Brandes emphasizes Ibsen's early preoccupation with the relation of father and son. It appears notably in *John Gabriel Borkman* where the pleasure-loving young Erhard will be neither a redeeming genius nor a family wage-earner. Repudiating all 'castellar' claims, he will go out into the wide world with the partner of his choice.

Stressing such points is superfluous; it is more trivial still to pick out other personal details from Ibsen's biography. Yet, aware of Joyce's curious interest in correspondences between himself and his friends, I confess myself struck by the parallels between Ibsen's early ambition to be a painter and Joyce's to be a singer; by their reaction from a short-lived bohemianism in dress to their natural, almost exaggerated, neatness; and by their appeals, when in an emergency, in the one case to the Swedish and in the other to the British crown. To escape such further entanglements I revert to Joyce's Italian reading at college when he was first translating his life into literature.

What really mattered was that he continued at college the Italian he had begun at Belvedere. He grew to love that language and literature so that when, later, he resolved to leave Dublin, it was choice more than chance that led him to Italy rather than to Scandinavia or France. Italian had become, in effect, his second language. He liked speaking it, he loved the sonority of its vocables and the grace and precision of its classics. His Italian class in college was, indeed, the only one he followed with any pretence at assiduity and the texts with which he grew acquainted there from 1899 to 1902 included Tasso, Machiavelli, Maffei, Monti, Manzoni, Petrarch, Castiglione, Dante, and Leopardi. He encountered them more or less in that order. From one or two of them I pick up some threads which seem to tie up, however tenuously, with his early experience.

Leopardi, for example, was included in his 1901 course. This was the year before his Mangan paper and Leopardi is introduced into that discourse by way of contrast with the Irish poet and as a spirit stronger than his—a heroic pessimist with the patience and courage of his own despair. Joyce presented Mangan in his home as a sensitive boy living amid much coarseness and misery. Would Joyce at the same time have remembered that Leopardi also was the victim of a family despot and lived under the sway of what Stephen Dedalus was to call 'castellar rights'? And would he have found in the poet's father, as I like to think, another and more sympathetic trait? Joyce used to say that he would sooner be Lord Mayor of his city than head of the State. Count Monaldo Leopardi reckoned a man's pride should not extend beyond his town. 'One's patriotism', he wrote, 'is not due to the whole nation, not even to the state; one's true country is only that morsel of the earth in which one is born and spends one's life. That alone should awaken any interest in its citizens.[1] In spite of his D'Annunzian ambition to forge a new conscience for his race, could not Joyce, here, have found something to confirm his dedication to his native city, as indeed also in a text of Edmund Burke which he was reading in the same year wherein Burke's wider comprehension could still find a place for 'attachment to the sub-division, the love of the little platoon we belong to'?

In his reading of the history of Italian literature he would, of course, have met the names of Giordano Bruno and Vico; but, though his feelers may have been stretching out in their direction, I see small evidence in those years of any real familiarity with their

[1] Iris Origo, *Leopardi* (London, 1935), p. 2.

work. I refer later to a sonnet attributed to the former, but with that possible exception I do not think he was reading consecutively, or, indeed, at all, in any of the characteristic texts of these very divergent philosophers. Such deliberately casual allusions as he made to Bruno he could have gathered in plenty, and he was plainly held and horrified, as by every instance of barbarism, by the Nolan's tragic destiny. But, notwithstanding the genuine feeling, eloquence, and youthful parade exhibited in the article he devoted to Bruno in 1903, I see no proof of any wide, textual acquaintance. On the other hand, in 1901 he was reading Fornaciari's *Disegno Storico della Letteratura Italiana* as part of his college course and even in that slender outline—apart from other sources—the references to Bruno and to Vico, to the intuitional and pantheistic mode of Bruno's thinking, to the indeterminate, encyclopedic sweep of mind which makes Vico, as Fornaciari says, an inexhaustible mine for future quarrying are sufficient to set an intelligence less alert than Joyce's upon inquiry. At any rate, Joyce alludes twice to Bruno in 1901 in 'The Day of the Rabblement' and again, more obscurely, in his Mangan paper of 1902, as well as (yet more doubtfully) to Vico. Passages in that paper treat as one the poetic and the philosophic vision and Joyce defends, as against the historian, poetry's intuitional approach to reality. In its closing sentences, where he invokes the vast courses which enfold us and a memory greater and more generous than our memory, one may feel a current deriving as much from Vico's cyclic view of history and from his *sapienza volgare* as from the theosophic airs which, in those days, were blowing about A.E. and Yeats. If this is so, the circle from 'Mangan' to *Finnegans Wake* over which Vico presides, already begins to be drawn.

This paper on Mangan is the most noteworthy memorial we have from Joyce's college years. It is a significant reminder of his struggling idealism, reflecting through the images it calls up the writer's attempt to arm himself with patient fortitude against difficult days crowding upon him. Other comfort and promptings he might have won from Machiavelli. There was more to this unlikely name than 'the dull, wooden words' of his 'dingy chronicle' falling piecemeal from Stephen's lips. There was in Machiavelli the irony which De Sanctis called his real muse and to this Joyce would willingly bend an attentive ear. And he had also perhaps for Joyce, at this moment, if not for Stephen Dedalus, something more than irony. To externalize the crudities of life, to set them down in all their harshness, is one way

by which the writer vindicates the supremacy of the spirit. And so
Joyce who, as I have said in an earlier chapter, had seen Baudelaire's
swan lifting its plumage from the soiling mud of the city, might in
his grievous hours have recalled words from the Florentine's self-
story: 'And wrapped in that baseness I take my brain out of the mud
and let the malignity of this fate of mine burst out of me, being glad
that it should trample on me like this, just to see if it can be ashamed of
itself.'[1]

These are speculations and we end them again with Bruno whom
he had invoked in 1901 as one who would have the lover of the good
and the true abhor the multitude and again in 1903 as one who had
cast away tradition. When Joyce came to write the *Portrait of the
Artist* he could have found in him, as I imagine, promptings, images,
or allegories as urgent. In the sonnet attributed to Bruno, 'Poi che
spiegate', he could have met Ovid's man and the son of Daedalus.

Bruno's name appears in the pages which end the *Portrait of the
Artist*. In its last sentences Stephen Dedalus feels the air thick with
the company of his kinsmen and their voices calling to him, making
ready for flight, shaking the wings of their exultant and terrible
youth. Is it not possible after this juxtaposition of Bruno's name to
overhear in these closing sentences the words of Bruno's sonnet as it
proceeds:

> Out on the air I hear the voice of my heart saying, 'Whither dost thou
> carry me, thou fearless one': And the answer, 'Fear not, though utter ruin
> should come to thee. Hold to the clouds and if thou die, be happy that
> Heaven has destined thee to so glorious a death.'

---

[1] De Sanctis, *History of Italian Literature* (trans. Joan Redfern, London, 1932),
vol. 2, p. 571. May we regard this as a whisper from 'old Nichiabelli's monolook
interyerear?' (*Finnegans Wake*, p. 182.)

INDEX